THE LAST OF THE GRAND HOTELS

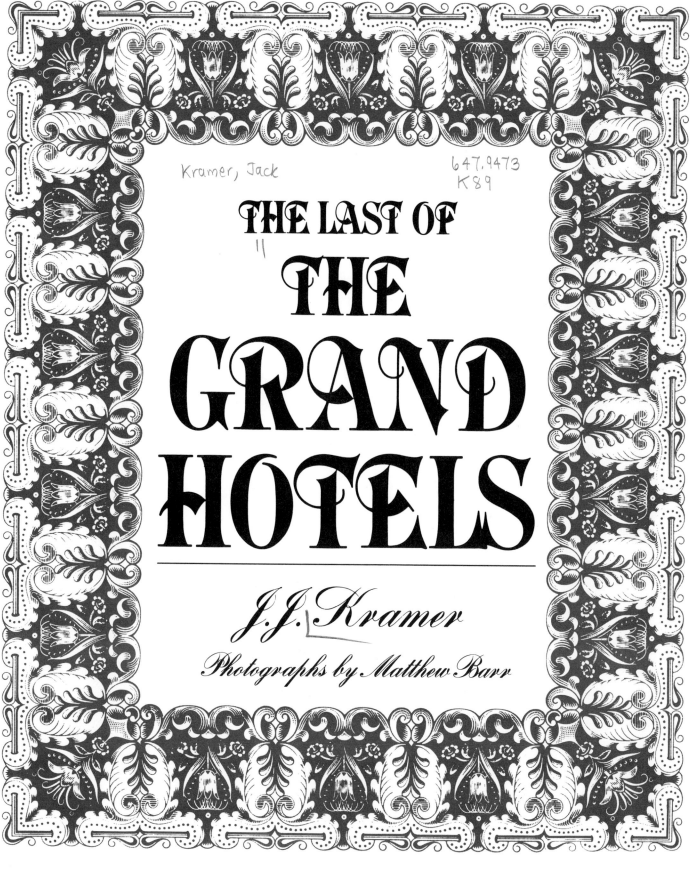

THE LAST OF
THE
GRAND
HOTELS

J.J. Kramer

Photographs by Matthew Barr

 VAN NOSTRAND REINHOLD COMPANY

NEW YORK   CINCINNATI   TORONTO   LONDON   MELBOURNE

COPYRIGHT © 1978 BY J. J. KRAMER
LIBRARY OF CONGRESS CATALOG CARD NUMBER 78-15690
ISBN 0-442-20819-7

PRINTED IN THE UNITED STATES OF AMERICA

PUBLISHED IN 1978 BY VAN NOSTRAND REINHOLD COMPANY
A DIVISION OF LITTON EDUCATIONAL PUBLISHING, INC.
135 WEST 50TH STREET, NEW YORK, NY 10020, U.S.A.

VAN NOSTRAND REINHOLD LIMITED
1410 BIRCHMOUNT ROAD
SCARBOROUGH, ONTARIO M1P 2E7, CANADA

VAN NOSTRAND REINHOLD AUSTRALIA PTY. LTD.
17 QUEEN STREET
MITCHAM, VICTORIA 3132, AUSTRALIA

VAN NOSTRAND REINHOLD COMPANY LIMITED
MOLLY MILLARS LANE
WORKINGHAM, BERKSHIRE, ENGLAND

1 3 5 7 9 11 13 15 16 14 12 10 8 6 4 2

LIBRARY OF CONGRESS CATALOGING IN PUBLICATION
KRAMER, JACK, 1927-
    THE LAST OF THE GRAND HOTELS.

    INCLUDES INDEX.
    1. HOTELS, TAVERNS, ETC.—UNITED STATES—HISTORY.
I. BARR, MATTHEW. II. TITLE.
TX909.K73   647 .9473   78-15690
ISBN 0-442-20819-7

BOOK DESIGN BY JEAN CALLAN KING/VISUALITY

Acknowledgments

Because I contacted so many people connected with the hotels included in this book it would be impossible to thank each one by name. Rather, I offer to all the employees of the Grand Hotels my collective thanks for their cooperation and help in this project.

I also want to thank Robert Carmack for his enthusiasm and valued assistance. He diligently researched a great deal of the material for this book and helped read copy and made suggestions as well.

To Helen van Pelt Wilson my sincere thanks and gratitude again for reading and rereading the manuscript and making the valuable suggestions that brought it to its finished form.

And to Marguerite Allen of the Warner Hotel Association I offer a big thank you. Her cooperation in this project was beyond the call of duty.

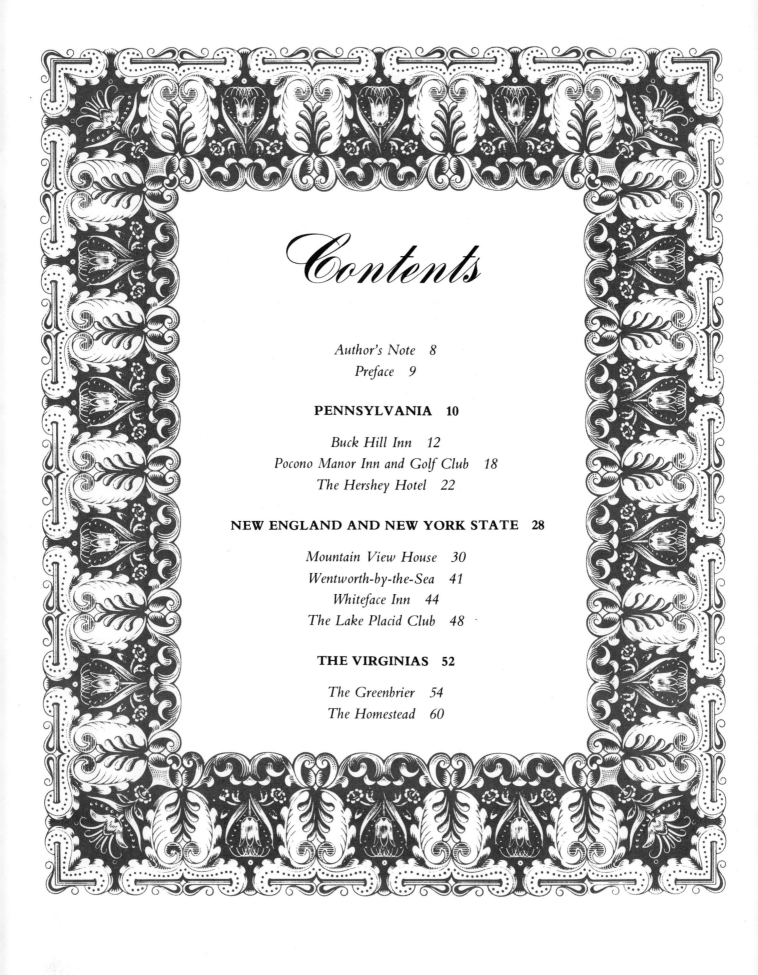

Contents

Author's Note

It would be impossible in one book to explore the glories of all the grand hotels and resorts in the United States. For this book it was decided to narrow our scope to concentrate on country and resort-type establishments; city hotels of stature have not been included.

The mention of a specific hotel in the book should in no way be considered an endorsement. This is a pictorial history, not a critical treatise. We limited our coverage to those hotels we were able to photograph personally, so if your favorite spa is missing it is purely through the exigencies of space and time.

Preface

The grandeur of yesterday can still be found today; but, like so much that is beautiful, it exists in a world apart. Sequestered in scenic areas of the United States, there stand, still proud and majestic, the last of the Grand Hotels. For many vacationers, a taste of the luxury of a bygone era is a pleasure today, perhaps as remembrance of a better time or perhaps because the Grand Hotels really are grand and remain the best and most splendid of retreats. In stately public rooms, amidst opulent accommodations and lushly landscaped grounds, we are more apt to forget the concrete and confusion of the city.

Built mainly in the latter part of the Nineteenth and early decades of the Twentieth Centuries, the Grand Hotels reflect an era of prosperity. War and depression were around the corner, but few knew it. The models for these hotels were the great resorts and spas of Europe. Architecturally, the Renaissance *palazzi* of Italy and the manors, *chateaux,* and *castillos* of the golden ages of England, France, and Spain served as inspiration. Alas, today's building costs have rendered such fine appointments and craftsmanship impossible to duplicate. What stands now is all we have.

The economic and social history of the period of the grand resorts has been explored in other books, most notably *Great Resorts of North America,* by Andrew Hepburn, and *Last Resorts,* by Cleveland Amory. Here, we offer a pictorial record and brief history of what once was and what remains today—a remembrance of America at the height of its luxury.

J. J. Kramer

PENNSYLVANIA

About a hundred miles from New York and from Philadelphia, just west of the Delaware Water Gap, the Pocono Mountains begin their gentle ascent. In 1870 the charm of this forested area was known to few—the Poconos were largely inaccessible, and they suffered in comparison to such majestic ranges as the Adirondacks of New York State and the White Mountains of New England. Few vacationers at that time looked toward Pennsylvania.

It was the Quakers, specifically Samuel Griscom of Philadelphia, who saw the possibilities of these unfrequented mountains as a place of quiet retreat in a favorable climate that was neither very hot nor very cold. Under his leadership the Society of Friends in Philadelphia organized a company, bought land, and made plans to establish a summer colony in the Poconos.

A key element in the development of the Pocono resorts was the expansion of the railroads. It is fortunate that the increase in prosperity within the Quaker community and their desire to vacation in congenial surroundings coincided with the burgeoning of the Railroad Age. As soon as the railroads came through and access roads were built, the first of the great Pocono resorts was born.

That establishment, now known as Buck Hill Inn but originally referred to as The Inn at Buck Hill Falls, was so successful that in 1902 another group of Quakers decided to build a second colony and guest lodge in the Poconos. Not so prosperous at first as Buck Hill, but in equally beautiful environs, it was named Pocono Manor.

There is perhaps some irony in the fact that the height of the Poconos' popularity as a family resort area coincided so closely with the golden age of rail travel, and that its decline as such came in tandem with decline of the railroads and the subsequent rise of the motor car. Today the Poconos, still enormously popular with vacationers, is best known as "The Honeymoon Capital of the United States." And the great resorts have found a new clientele among corporations, for whom the epic proportions and large-scale facilities are ideally suited for conventions and sales meetings.

The Hershey Hotel in southern Pennsylvania is of yet another age and another tradition. Built in the Thirties and the product of one man's fertile imagination, it is a monument of a peculiarly American sort. The town of Hershey was hardly ideal for a large resort—it boasts no mountains, no lakes in the immediate vicinity, few tourist attractions. But Milton S. Hershey decided that an elegant resort was a necessity in his town; The Hershey Hotel stands today to do him honor.

Buck Hill Inn

BUCK HILL FALLS, PENNSYLVANIA

A Philadelphia Quaker named Samuel Griscom had inherited from his father a tract of several thousand acres of wilderness in eastern Pennsylvania. So taken was he with the beauty of the area that he tried to interest other members of the Quaker community in establishing a summer retreat there. Howard M. Jenkins, editor of the *Friends Intelligencer,* was less enthusiastic than Griscom but he consented to make a visit before passing judgment on the idea.

In the late summer of 1900, Jenkins and his three sons, along with an associate named Henry Paiste, set off to view Griscom's claimed paradise. Getting there was, in those days, by no means easy. The trip began by train. The party met at Trenton and changed there for the Delaware Valley Railroad, which carried the five men to the end of the line at Manunka Chunk. There they waited for a train of the Delaware, Lackawanna, and Western Railroad. (This was known familiarly as the D. L. and W., which many claimed stood for Delay, Linger, and Wait. In fairness to the railroad it should be noted that by 1902 reliable once-a-day service had been established.) The train deposited them at Cresco station, from which they were driven to Henry Price's boarding house to spend the night. In the morning the patience of the visiting gentlemen was rewarded as they viewed the magnificent Buck Hill Falls—actually two waterfalls plummeting over 200 feet through a rocky ravine—and the surrounding countryside. Jenkins was convinced.

That autumn, a corporation was formed to develop a vacation retreat; Harold M. Jenkins was one of the officers, and the Philadelphia architectural firm of Bunting and Shrigley was engaged to design the guest lodge and grounds. The plan was to sell stock to members of the Friends community who wished to build vacation cottages on the property; community activities would center around a main lodge, which would serve also to accommodate visitors and guests of community members.

The location of the Inn was paramount, and in such an overwhelmingly beautiful setting there were several possibilities. Finally, the shoulder of Buck Hill was chosen. There the building would receive the breeze from three sides and the acreage around it would provide ideal sites for the cottages.

Construction of the Inn and three cottages was well under way in June 1901, and it was promised that the Inn would be ready to receive guests in July. Progress was regularly reported in the *Friends Intelligencer.* The opening was pushed up to June 22. On that day, however, carpenters were still at work and the trunks of the twenty-one guests had to be carried up staircases still under construction. The original Inn had no private baths, no heat, and only kerosene lamps for lighting.

On October 19 the Inn closed its first season with guests reluctant to leave, so delightful had been their stay. The venture was considered a great success, and in December the corporation voted to enlarge the Inn. (On January 18, 1902, another branch of the Society of Friends announced plans to build an inn and country retreat along the model of Buck Hill. This was to be Pocono Manor.)

The Inn at Buck Hill Falls prospered and cottages multiplied in number and size. Some of the cottages were quite grand themselves, with thirty and forty rooms—hardly what we would today call a "cottage"! Over the next decade there were many additions and improvements to the property, including a sewage disposal system and an electrical plant.

The atmosphere was relaxing and understated, as befits a resort established and maintained under the aegis of the Society of Friends. A friend of mine who was a guest there in the 1920s recalls the gracious, low-key atmosphere of the family resort: There was always a

Facing page, sitting on the crest of Buck Hill, the Inn commands a spectacular view of the surrounding woodland. (Photo: The Scheller Company)

roaring fire in the lounge fireplace on cold mornings; cottages stretched along the road to the Inn; nature walks, especially to the Falls, were a popular activity, as were golf and tennis. (Bill Tilden played there at the time.) There was no ostentation. My friend, who was visiting in the company of her parents, recalls that her father donned a tuxedo for dinner their first night there but retreated in considerable embarrassment to change to the more casual clothes that prevailed in the dining room. Alcohol was forbidden in the public rooms; guests who wanted to play cards did so in their bedrooms; and on Sunday nearly everyone attended Friends Meeting in the East Room of the Inn.

Well managed by the Quakers to suit their philosophy and their notion of what a vacation resort should be, the Inn prospered. It was not until 1916 that a resolution was passed allowing cars to be driven to and from the public road to the cottages, though not up the drive to the Inn itself. Peace reigned.

Throughout the Twenties major renovations and new construction kept up with the growing popularity of Buck Hill. By 1923 there were more than 200 bedrooms in the Inn proper. The original frame buildings were gradually replaced, the last in 1930. New units were built with native stone, which harmonized with the terrain. A formal garden was planted behind the Inn, leading to a twenty-seven-hole golf course. Many trails ran through virgin forests, notably Jenkins Woods with its giant hemlocks and beyond which lay the spectacular Falls.

By the 1930s, visitors from all over the country were flocking to the Inn, and the most stringent of the Quaker rules were abandoned. Today, there is full bar service and the dining room offers an excellent selection of fine imported and domestic wines from a well-stocked cellar.

Buck Hill Inn is now the largest resort in the Poconos, secluded on 6,000 forested acres. The natural beauty of this year-round retreat has brought a devoted clientele of some half a million guests each year.

Although still very much connected with its history, Buck Hill Inn has been, since 1977, managed by a corporation formed to provide an administration separate from that of the residential cottage community, which nonetheless shares the surrounding land. The new corporation operates in harmony with the residual Buck Hill Falls Company, and the Inn remains an inviting prospect for family vacations, weekend retreats, and, thanks to its extensive facilities, corporate conferences.

Above, writing desks and informal conversational groupings contribute to the warm and relaxing atmosphere in the Exchange South, one of the several public rooms at Buck Hill Inn.

Below, the lustrously panelled East Room, once the Sunday meeting place for the Quakers who founded The Inn at Buck Hill Falls, is now used for chamber concerts, movies, banquets, or simply as a pleasant place to pass the time. (Photos: Richard Averill Smith)

Opposite, the north facade of Buck Hill Inn. The handsome stonework can be seen through blossoms of mountain laurel, Pennsylvania's state flower which is abundantly planted on the grounds of Buck Hill. (Photo: American Aerial Survey)

Pocono Manor Inn and Golf Club

POCONO, PENNSYLVANIA

Rising high above the banks of the Delaware River in this splendidly hilly area of eastern Pennsylvania, Pocono Manor Inn and Golf Club reflects its tranquil Quaker heritage. Like Buck Hill Inn, Pocono Manor began at a "called" meeting of Friends in Philadelphia. The idea was to purchase a tract of land in the Pocono Mountains to provide a place where the Quakers could relax away from the city and enjoy their own quiet way of life. The beauty of the surroundings—verdant forests and clear waters—was appropriate to the Quaker emphasis on peacefulness and simplicity in a natural setting. With the railroad extending ever closer to these once remote areas, a resort seemed a feasible project. And so it was.

On April 15, 1902, construction began on a small summer lodge, and by August it was ready to accept its first guests. During the first six years of its existence, the resort operated only in the summer and early fall. In 1908, a winter facility was added and Pocono Manor thus became one of the first year-round resorts in the Poconos.

Within a few years of its inception, the resort grew to nearly 3,000 acres through purchases of surrounding land. As the years passed, private vacation cottages sprang up and a handsome colony developed along with the Manor. In 1925, an eight-story 106-room addition was made to the main lodge, bringing the total to 280 rooms. The resort prospered.

The 1925 construction was, however, the last for almost half a century; the Manor continued thereafter as a popular resort but neither additions nor improvements were made. Time took its toll of the buildings and, even in its beautiful surroundings, the establishment suffered.

In 1967, Samuel W. Ireland of Atlantic City's Coffee-Tea Inc., purchased the resort. His wife Beatrice noted that "Everything was brown and rundown. Floors slanted so badly in some places it seemed you were walking on a rocking ship." The Irelands embarked on a ten-year, $3-million renovation, with Mr. Ireland directing repairs and Mrs. Ireland supervising the redecoration in an Early American style. New lounges were comfortably furnished with sofas and deep chairs. Extensive structural alterations provided fifteen meeting rooms, for up to seventy persons. The buildings were completely rewired, new water storage and fire systems were installed. All the windows were replaced, the bathrooms were handsomely modernized, and thirty-two new guest rooms added. The Plymouth Meeting Center was built and an enclosed walkway connected it with the Manor. The Pro Shop and Golf House Restaurant were expanded, and an outdoor free-form pool was built with an extensive sun deck. All rooms are air-conditioned.

In 1975 a ski lodge was completed; snowmaking equipment and a second ski lift now provide full season skiing at its best. The following year four all-weather tennis courts were added, bringing the number of courts to nine. Today outdoor activities include skiing, ice-skating, snowmobiling, and sleigh and toboggan riding in winter, and tennis, golf, trout fishing, and hay rides in summer.

Six employees supervise the social programs and, according to the hotel's management, 50 of its 200 employees have been at Pocono Manor for more than twenty-five years. Although the Manor caters to groups of 6 to 600, it always has its share of honeymooners. Mindful that the Pocono area is famous as the "Honeymoon Capital of the United States," the Inn has added a honeymoon trail, where couples may select a personal tree and have it marked with a nameplate and date.

Facing page, recently redecorated in an Early American motif, the interior of Pocono Manor Inn is cozy and comfortable.

Above, venerable shade trees and tidy green lawns are part of the landscaping at Pocono Manor.

Below, the dining room at Pocono Manor.

Opposite, guests relax at poolside. The buildings of Pocono Manor are distinguished by a graceful marriage of stone, brick, and wood.

In 1977, Pocono Manor celebrated its seventy-fifth anniversary. Situated on 3,100 acres with more than 300 guest rooms and cottages, the Manor is today in splendid condition and handsomely furnished in Colonial style. Dominated by a gabled clock tower topped with a weathervane, the main buildings consist of three five-story wings and a modern eight-story addition. And although much has changed since 1902, it remains a gracious retreat amidst the glories of nature—forests, mountains, and rushing rivers.

The Hershey Hotel

HERSHEY, PENNSYLVANIA

The history of The Hershey Hotel in the Pennsylvania Dutch country reads like the great American success story. And, indeed, it is intimately tied up with the life of one of this country's most dramatically successful, if more than a little bit eccentric, businessmen. The man is Milton Snavely Hershey (1857–1945) and the story begins in 1893, in neighboring Lancaster, Pennsylvania, where Hershey situated his first chocolate factory and set out to produce the best chocolate bar at the lowest price. In 1904, with twelve families and a deed to 300 acres of cornfields, Hershey moved his factory and built a town around it. Hershey, Pennsylvania, was the result. Not quite thirty years later, in 1932, Hershey, by then many times a millionaire, decided to build himself, and his town, a hotel. If visions of Kubla Khan and his stately pleasure dome come to mind, the reader will not be too far afield.

It was Mrs. Hershey who suggested that the building be modeled after The Heliopolis Hotel in Cairo. By the time ground was broken, however, the Heliopolis plans proved too expensive. Undaunted, Mr. Hershey directed architect and chief engineer D. Paul Whitmer to use as his model a Mediterranean hotel that resembled a Spanish *castillo*. He offered Whitmer a picture postcard of said hotel as the source from which to draw his blueprints.

Construction, begun in the mild winter of 1932, was completed in late spring, 1933.

Lowell Thomas once described the Hotel as "A palace, a palace that out-palaces the palaces of the mararajahs of India." The architectural style can be best described as eclectic, with an emphasis on Spanish and Moorish elements. The Hotel lobby resembles a Spanish patio, with a working fountain in the center, inlaid tile floor, wall hangings, oak-paneled ceiling and columns, and a commemorative mural of life in old Spain. The Spanish-style dining room, a huge and airy semicircle, looks out upon the gardens and the mountains beyond.

The dining room, in fact, is a tale in itself and perhaps the best example of how Milton Hershey's peculiar requirements shaped the character of the Hotel more than any architect's vision could have. The room features thirteen clear glass windows surrounded by stained glass designs showing vines, birds, and butterflies. From the beamed ceiling hang wrought-iron chandeliers. The challenge presented to the architect was that the room was to have no interior columns. As the story goes, Hershey was once seated behind a pillar in a restaurant and was so annoyed that he vowed that when he built *his* hotel no diner would have to suffer the same indignity.

But if Milton Hershey was an eccentric, he was also a humanitarian who did more with his millions than spend them for his private pleasures. Evidence of his largesse can be seen at the Hotel and environs.

The Hershey Industrial School is the most richly endowed orphanage and vocational school in the world. Hershey began it in 1905, and in 1918 bestowed $60 million to it. The school is today the chief beneficiary and controlling stockholder of both the chocolate conglomerate and the Hotel.

The story of the fabulous gardens on the grounds of the Hotel is no less impressive.

In 1936, Milton Hershey was asked for $1 million to establish a national rosarium near Washington, D.C. A man clearly filled with local pride and civic consciousness, Hershey replied that he preferred to spend the money locally. In cooperation with the Garden Club Federation of Pennsylvania, he planned a three-and-a-half-acre formal rose garden, to be built on the Hotel grounds but open to the public. The site was selected by Harry Erdman, manager

Facing page, the leaded and stained glass windows in the dining room of The Hershey Hotel frame the natural beauty of the view outside and add to it their own crafted loveliness.

of the landscaping division of Hershey estates. Construction began in early July 1936 on the side of the high knoll on which the Hotel stands. Water pipes and electrical conduits for lighting were laid, a deeply eroded gully was turned into Swan Lake, which served not only to check storm runoff but to provide irrigation for the garden.

In November the first planting of 12,500 roses in 112 varieties was undertaken. The gardens were opened to throngs of visitors in late May 1937. On the first June weekend after the opening, more than 20,000 visitors came in a single day. In the course of the next three years the number of rose varieties was increased to 700, and more than 13,000 rose plants were set out.

By 1941, with more than 500,000 visitors annually, Hershey added an adjoining seventeen-acre tract and had it landscaped with trees and shrubs, a collection of rare evergreens and flowers, and, of course, more roses—a total of 38,000. Today the gardens cover more than twenty-three acres and include some 120,000 plants.

Perched atop the highest hill in the area, the resort looks much the same today as it did in 1933. The $2.2-million West Wing, opened in 1977, blends with the stone walls and tiled roofs of the original building. Some changes in decor have been made through the years and

The reflecting pool and formal gardens impart a classical quality to the grounds of The Hershey Hotel.

The Hershey Hotel is a sprawling structure with a character all its own. It is a blend of architectural types combined to create an extraordinary edifice.

new facilities have been added: a cocktail bar, a nine-hole golf course, a grand ballroom, a wine cellar, and meeting rooms of various sizes. In 1961 a swimming pool was cut into the hillside in the midst of a pine grove and in 1968 the garden-patio-dining area was added.

The old wing now has 150 rooms, the West Wing 120; all are climate-controlled and offer splendid vistas of the formal gardens and spacious rolling lawns. There are two dining rooms, two championship eighteen-hole golf courses, five tennis courts, an outdoor and an indoor swimming pool, and hiking, horseback, and cycling trails.

Bedrooms are open to both morning and afternoon sunlight and are tastefully decorated in a range of styles—Early American, French, Spanish, Italian, English, and Georgian. The central section of the Hotel opens onto a wide sun terrace with a view of the Hershey domain. A classically elegant reflecting pool adds to the grandeur of it all.

A community of 9,000 people, Hershey, Pennsylvania, offers to visitors not only the world's largest chocolate factory but a museum of American life, a high meadow camp, an amusement park that rivals Disneyland, and a Chocolate World exhibition hall. The Hershey Hotel, far from being Milton Hershey's folly, is the town's link with its past and a splendid showplace for visitors from all over the world.

Above, in the foreground the reflecting pool; beyond it the Mediterranean character of The Hershey is splendidly evident.

Below, this lobby area at The Hershey, with its tile inlaid floor and fountain, has a Spanish air about it.

The spacious dining room at The Hershey. By Milton Hershey's decree, there are no pillars or other supports to obstruct the view. Window tables look past the garlands of stained glass flowers and out onto the beautifully landscaped grounds.

NEW ENGLAND AND NEW YORK STATE

The six states of New England and neighboring New York State encompass within their borders a dramatic range of geographical wonders—from mountain heights to sandy seashore, from alpine lakes to the Atlantic surf, and all the rolling foothills and lush green valleys that run between. The area was among the first settled in Colonial times and it has continued to be a major population center for several hundred years since then. It should, then, be no wonder that the area would be dotted also with grand resorts, both at the seaside and in the mountains.

In New England, the shore was the prime resort locale in the Nineteenth Century. Winter sports were far in the future; the cooling and healthful sea air as respite from the humid inland summer was what vacationers sought in those days. Between 1870 and 1900 New England's coastline bloomed with sprawling wooden buildings. Supposedly Victorian in design, most looked more like a carpenter's nightmare—but every one commanded a fine view of the ocean. These monoliths hugged every promontory and offered a formal atmosphere in which service and elegance were paramount. Most of these wooden giants are gone, victims of fire or bankruptcy. (Summer resorts could not make enough money in three months to carry them through twelve.)

One that did survive the decades, and in splendid style, is Wentworth-by-the-Sea, a showcase of Victorian elegance on the New Hampshire coast. An establishment of a very different sort is Mountain View House, which perches at the foot of the Presidential Range of New Hampshire's White Mountains, exemplifying the dramatic transition from shoreline to timberline that New England can offer.

Moving southwest from the New England mountains, the traveler arrives in New York State. Surrounded by forest and girdled by mountain peaks, Lake Placid is an ideal resort setting, and two great hotels share that lake shore—Whiteface Inn and The Lake Placid Club.

The Adirondacks that lace more than 8,000 square miles of New York State offer gorgeous scenery and the good fresh air sadly lacking in large cities. Despite the general hotel boom during the 1870s to 1900s and the area's proximity to New York City, Boston, and Buffalo, it took more than money to make the Adirondacks inviting. The splendid setting was a factor, but more important was the conviction of many physicians that the climate of the Adirondack region was helpful in treating tuberculosis, consumption, and other respiratory ailments. As Europeans went to take the waters, Americans went to take the air. And, in the course of time, they went to Whiteface Inn and The Lake Placid Club.

Today, the Adirondacks are a four-season resort area, assuring the future of its hotels. The enormous popularity of skiing, both downhill and cross-country, as well as other cold weather outdoor activities, has given the region a long-term lease on life.

Mountain View House

WHITEFIELD, NEW HAMPSHIRE

Mountain View House, as it stands today, is a far cry from its humble beginning as a four-room farmhouse on the crest of a hill in northern New Hampshire. William Franklin Dodge built the farmhouse in the mid-1800s. The Dodges were hospitable people. In 1864, as the story goes, a stagecoach broke down en route to some destination now forgotten; while the coach was undergoing repairs, the travelers were housed at the Dodge farm. They found the environs so inviting and the hospitality so disarming that they sent on the coach and stayed for quite a while. The next year the travelers returned with friends. Thus was born in William Franklin Dodge's mind the idea of converting his farm to an inn. He called it Mountain View House. Today the inn is a handsome, gleaming white building that offers superb cuisine and service to countless guests.

Word spread quickly and people began coming from all over New England, attracted by its reputation for exceptionally good food and a beautiful location. As greater numbers of travelers discovered the resort, additions were made to the farmhouse. With the completion of each new structure, the mortgage was burned with due ceremony by the Dodge family. The farm provided the inn kitchen with milk, chickens, and fresh vegetables, and Mary Jane Dodge was a fine cook and a peerless housekeeper.

In 1884, Van Herbert Dodge, one of the two Dodge sons, took over management of the hotel. The original four-room farmhouse was incorporated into a larger frame building, which itself continued to be expanded. Year by year improvements were made. When Van Dodge died in 1934, his son, Frank Schuyler Dodge, took over; under this third generation of Dodge management the hotel continued to be a first-class summer resort. Frank had married Mary Eunice Bowden in 1927, and husband and wife together ran the resort until March 1948, when Frank died. Mary took over management for five years until Frank Schuyler, Jr., was of age and ready to take the reins of the now very popular Mountain View House.

Mary Bowden Dodge was remarried in 1953 to Professor Thomas W. Silk, who as a young man had been an employee of the hotel. Tom became hotel treasurer and helped update the auditing system. Through his efforts the business continued to grow and prosper.

There is little left of the original Dodge farm, but the resort is still owned by the family. The main building is remembered for its dramatic, square tower that faces south. The building is now four stories high and has several wings. Sweeping lawns provide a rich green welcome; the grounds themselves are a plant lover's delight with hundreds of acres of informal gardens and meadows filled with wildflowers.

At a time when most hotels, grand and otherwise are owned by large corporations, Mountain View House is perhaps unique—the line of ownership and management has stayed within a single family from its inception to the present day.

Facing page, originally a small farmhouse, Mountain View House has been extended through a succession of white clapboard wings, each addition made as the hotel's popularity increased and, with it, the need for space.

Left, the clerestory windows and pillars make the dining room at Mountain View House a light and airy space.

Below, the veranda at Mountain View House offers both sun and shade, and of course, a breathtaking view of the White Mountains of New England.

BUCK HILL INN

Above, the north facade of Buck Hill Inn, framed in evergreens and mountain laurel. The roundstone exterior remains much the same as when it was originally built in the 1920s. (Photo: The Scheller Company)

Left, lawn bowling has been a favorite pastime at Buck Hill for decades. The meticulously groomed turf, shown here in an aerial view, is the frequent site of national lawn bowling championship tournaments. (Photo: The Scheller Company)

POCONO MANOR INN AND GOLF CLUB

Facing page, the swimming pool at Pocono Manor, added as part of the renovation undertaken in the later 1960s. Note the handsome clock tower that caps the centermost of the Manor's three wings.

Right, one of the guest cottages on the grounds at Pocono Manor. Originally built as private vacation dwellings by the Quakers who founded Pocono Manor, these cottages today serve as luxuriously isolated accommodations.

Below, the charming lobby at Pocono Manor. The renovation of the past decade included a full transformation of the interior to an Early American decor.

THE HERSHEY HOTEL

Facing page, top, The Hershey Hotel viewed from the side. The handsome reflecting pool accents the elegance of the lawns that surround the Hotel.

Facing page, bottom, the Moorish inspiration for The Hershey Hotel is evident in this view of the facade. Arched windows and porticoes are complemented by the tile roofs.

This page, a glimpse of Milton Hershey's multi-million-dollar gardens. A major attraction for visitors from all parts of the country, the gardens encompass over twenty-three acres. This formal arrangement offers a view of the golf links and more distant woods.

This page, The Hershey Hotel lobby, with its fountain, tiled floor, and arched porticoes, establishes the flavor of Old Spain at first sweeping glance.

MOUNTAIN VIEW HOUSE

Facing page, top, from the outside, the simple New England elegance of Mountain View House is evident. The belvedere tower and the dormer windows in the upper-story rooms provide the view that gives the hotel its name.

Facing page, bottom, beautiful flowers, seasonal potted plants, and stately old trees are a stroller's delight on the grounds of Mountain View House.

Following page, the colonnaded veranda provides a relaxing ambience for hotel guests, whether they are seeking sun or shade, or, later, a bit of night air.

Wentworth-by-the-Sea

NEW CASTLE, NEW HAMPSHIRE

Preceding page, the facade of Wentworth-by-the-Sea, with its central tower and widow's walk, a classic feature of New England seaside architecture.

This page, the beautifully appointed lobby area.

Facing page, wooden steps and walkway lead down from the sprawling white buildings and out to the beach.

With cupolas and brightly colored slate roofs, Wentworth-by-the-Sea in New Castle, New Hampshire, commands a view of both river and ocean, a rare offering in an otherwise landlocked state. Surrounded on three sides by the Piscataqua River, the hotel rises majestically from the seashore just north of Portsmouth, a treasure of high Victoriana.

The celebrated Wentworth is one of the many grand resort hotels that sprang up in the decade following the Civil War. Named after Benning Wentworth, one-time royal governor of New Hampshire who lived in New Castle, the building was started in 1873 by Charles E. Campbell, who owned the land, and Daniel Chase, who handled the financing. In 1897, a Portsmouth man by the name of Frank Jones bought The Wentworth and added the third story, the towers, and the dining room wing. Between 1902 and the outbreak of World War II, The Wentworth changed hands several times and underwent expansion and improvement, including the addition of bowling alleys, a bathhouse, swimming pool, golf course, and tennis courts. It was in the Twenties that the name itself was expanded to Wentworth-by-the-Sea.

Like most hotels of its era, Wentworth-by-the-Sea has had its share of notable visitors, but perhaps the most impressive moment in its history occurred in 1905, when the hotel hosted the treaty negotiations that ended the Russo-Japanese War. Worldwide newspaper coverage focused on the hotel. Today it is still popular as a center for conventions and meetings.

During World War II, the hotel was closed, as were so many other grand resorts, the attention of the country having turned to concerns other than leisure. It reopened, under the new ownership of the James Barker Smiths, in the summer of 1946. In the more than three decades since then, the Smiths have made numerous additions to bring the premises up to date with the requirements of today's clientele, which includes facilities for conventions and sales meetings.

Through the years, a number of architects and designers have had a hand in the development of the building's structure, and each successive owner has added his own taste and touch, frequently influenced by the hotels of Europe. But for all its varied heritage, Wentworth-by-the-Sea has a unified appearance. That each owner loved the hotel is evident in the meticulous attention to detail that characterizes its appearance and ambience.

The hotel has always had a gracious air, and of course it has its idyllic location. The site is the crest of a low ridge; the river is to the north, the ocean to the south. The happy marriage of land and water affords guests at Wentworth-by-the-Sea opportunities for boating and fishing. On a rocky beach fringed with tall pine trees, ovens have been installed for the popular clambakes the hotel sponsors. The clambakes draw immense crowds, and it is said that Wentworth-by-the-Sea serves more lobster than any other hotel in the country.

Whiteface Inn

LAKE PLACID, NEW YORK

The history of Whiteface Inn, a Gothic structure of epic proportions built in 1888, is linked with that of the Otis Elevator Company. It was Colonel A. G. Mills, vice-president of that company, who organized a group that purchased land overlooking Whiteface Mountain.

The Lake Placid region in the Adirondacks was just beginning to gain popularity as a fashionable resort center at the time Colonel Mills caught sight of it. The beauty of high mountain lakes combined with an agreeable climate was part of the attraction; the prescription of clean mountain air for sufferers from hay fever and respiratory ailments provided the rest.

Colonel Mills made a wise investment and the region gained a Grand Hotel. The first decade of the Twentieth Century was a prosperous period for resorts throughout the United States, Whiteface Inn being no exception. The portico-porched structure—with its 150 rooms it was large for its day—stood for twenty years until it was destroyed by fire in 1908. In 1912 a larger building was constructed on the same site, but fire struck again in 1917. By that time Whiteface Inn had changed hands. The new owners rebuilt the hotel in the basic plan it reflects today. Throughout the years, however, considerable remodeling has been undertaken.

In 1930, Henry Haynes, a Kentucky-born hotelier who had amassed a fortune in Florida resort properties, accepted the summer management of the Inn. He was so successful that he was offered a partnership in the company. From 1930 to 1955, Haynes almost single-handedly turned the hotel into a veritable palace with luxurious suites, spacious public rooms, and a splendid golf course. When Haynes' regime ended, the Inn was purchased by a syndicate headed by the experienced hotel manager F. Burton Fischer. (At this writing the ownership of Whiteface Inn is again in flux; its future depends on a court decision.)

Today, Whiteface Inn is a sprawling complex, with cottages, chalet, and a main lodge, covering more than 1,000 acres. The accommodations are as varied as they are comfortable. The lodge houses about 150 guests; the lake-front chalet has rooms for an additional 40, and more than forty attractive cottages face the lake shore.

The beauty of Whiteface Inn owes much, of course, to its location; sequestered as it is in the alpine splendor of forests and lake, it is a grand place to enjoy peace and quiet.

Facing page, the wooden structure of Whiteface Inn is an excellent example of a building type common in the early years of this century.

Whiteface Inn offers relaxation in a pastoral setting. Rustic cabins, the wood-frame main lodge, peaceful walking paths, informal plantings, and the surrounding forest lands make for a perfect harmony.

The Lake Placid Club

LAKE PLACID, NEW YORK

Located in the wooded ranges of the northeast corner of New York State, Lake Placid gleams like a blue jewel. What more perfect place could there be for an all-season grand resort hotel? So thought Melvil Dewey when he first laid eyes on the lake and surrounding mountains, and millions of vacationers since then have agreed.

Melvil Dewey is himself an interesting story, for reasons above and beyond his intuition about the Adirondacks, which, as we shall see, changed the complexion of America's leisurely pursuits. For he is the same man who developed the Dewey Decimal System, without which most libraries in the country would be considerably more chaotic than they are. A reformer in many areas—some more generally believed to be in need of reform than others—Melvil Dewey campaigned for simplified spelling, which extended to his name (he was born Melville) and the menu of his Lake Placid Club. He was also an ardent prohibitionist, but his attempts to exclude alcohol and tobacco from the resort proved unsuccessful.

Initially attracted to the area because of the clear mountain air, Dewey and his wife, hayfever sufferers in search of a restful spot for vacations, built a small farmhouse on the lake shore. In 1895, Dewey transformed that house into a clubhouse, named it The Lake Placid Club, and thus began what was to become the largest private resort hotel in the world. There were scoffers at first, largely because it was well known that as clear and salubrious as the mountain air might be, the vacation season in upper New York State was very short indeed. Undeterred, Dewey set out to introduce winter sports—including skiing, which was at the time virtually unknown on this side of the Atlantic.

Having assured his resort of a year-round clientele, Dewey set up The Lake Placid Club as a corporation, with participation as owners and operators limited to a few close friends. Throughout his lifetime, Dewey retained controlling interest in the Club, and upon his death in 1931, the majority stock, through a deed of gift, went into a nonprofit body now known as The Lake Placid Education Foundation.

From 1895 to 1900 visitors made the first leg of their journey, to Saranac Lake which lay ten miles to the west of Lake Placid, by train; they rode the rest of the way in horse-drawn carriages. By 1900 the railroad had extended a spur directly into the town of Lake Placid, and several years later overnight Pullman service to the Club was available from New York City.

The Club itself is a sprawling compound of buildings with a Queen Anne Period air about it. Guests are afforded splendid views of lake and mountains through the generous use of glass—the buildings feature many large picture windows, some of which have been there for more than fifty years, long before picture windows were in vogue. A local architect, William Distin of Saranac Lake, designed the main clubhouse unit, consisting of two wings known as the Agora Suite and the East Suite. Ronald Allwork, a New Yorker, designed the two later noncontiguous structures, the Golfhouse and Lakehouse.

A lot of water has flowed under the bridge since the first Lake Placid Club guests strapped wooden slats to their feet and sped off down a hill; for one thing, the Lake Placid region has become one of the major ski resort areas in the East. It has hosted one meeting of the Winter Olympics (in 1932) and is gearing up for a return visit in 1980. It is certainly fitting that The Lake Placid Club will be official Olympic headquarters.

Facing page, this sun-dappled terrace skirts the swimming pool at The Lake Placid Club.

This page, the pool from another angle. Behind it, the main Club building commands a stunning view of the Adirondacks.

Facing page, top, the greenhouse dining room at The Lake Placid Club mingles indoor and outdoor plantings.

Bottom, wood beams and picture windows grace this informal seating area in the lobby. The picture windows were an innovation when The Lake Placid Club was first built in the waning years of the Nineteenth Century.

THE VIRGINIAS

The Allegheny Mountain region of Virginia and West Virginia, which were until the Civil War the same state, is a land of forested mountains scored by pleasant valleys and clear rivers. In an area of about seventy-five square miles, which includes Virginia's Bath County, West Virginia's Greenbrier County, and several other counties in both states, mineral springs issue from deep below the earth's surface, warm and literally reeking with what many have believed for centuries to be curative elements.

The combination of the cool and pleasant mountain climate and the medicinal promise of the mineral springs has made this area an ideal locale for grand resort hotels and spas.

Since the 1700s the fertile tidal plains between the Potomac and York Rivers in Virginia have been dotted with tobacco plantations. As these plantations grew, so did the wealth of the owners, and the size of their mansions, and their taste for luxury. Unfortunately, mosquitoes also grew and prospered in the tidewater areas, making life uncomfortable, often unbearable in the heat of summer. Those who could afford it — and the plantation owners certainly could — looked to the west, to the Allegheny Mountains, for a cool summer retreat.

The first resort hotel was built in 1756; it stood on the site now occupied by the famed Homestead. The area developed rapidly. The wealth of the landed classes in the years before the Civil War, combined with the European-style of elegance in which these spas were run, made them very attractive indeed.

A physician named Thomas Goode was perhaps most instrumental in touting the medicinal benefits of the mineral springs; he advertised heavily, employing testimonials from guests who claimed to have been cured of a list of ailments running from dropsy to gout to lumbago.

Not surprisingly, the popularity of the area declined during the Civil War and in the period immediately following it. It was at that time that the western counties of Virginia, unable to support the secession of the eastern portion of the state, separated themselves and were admitted to the Union as the sovereign state of West Virginia. Its Confederate sister suffered badly in the war and the formerly wealthy landed class was in no condition to vacation in the manner to which it had become accustomed.

The resurgence of the area was due in large part to the purchase, by the Chesapeake and Ohio Railroad, of one of the two great hotels situated there, The Greenbrier. In a type of transaction that is still common today, the transportation industry joined forces with the hostelry industry to cash in on the public's desire for a change of scene. The Chesapeake and Ohio Railroad is now called Chessie System, Inc., but it still owns the hotel its rail line serves.

The Greenbrier
WHITE SULPHUR SPRINGS, WEST VIRGINIA

The Greenbrier, standing like a monument to the grand style, has a long and illustrious history. It began in 1778, when a woman named Amanda Anderson, after one submersion in the White Sulphur Springs, declared her rheumatism cured. The crowds which thereupon flocked to the site in the upper Allegheny Valley required a place to stay.

In 1794, sixteen years after Amanda Anderson's dip, Michael Bowyer constructed two rows of cottages at White Sulphur Springs. (These cottages are still in use today.) In 1809, Bowyer and an associate by the name of James Calwell built a two-story tavern. Seven years later the first private dwelling—it was called the President's Cottage, but remember, what folks meant by *cottage* in those days is closer to our idea of a mansion—was built in Federal style. Through the years more resort buildings sprang up in the area, and in 1858 The Grand Central Hotel, The Greenbrier's predecessor, opened for business. It came to be called The Old White Hotel, appropriately so as it was a massive white building four stories high and 400 feet long, complete with arcades and a Grecian dome.

The Old White prospered for several years. But with the start of the Civil War, the owners lost their financial backing. The Hotel was used for a time as a military hospital for both the Union and Confederate soldiers. After the war it was bought by a syndicate, which reopened it in 1866. Business was slow in the war-scarred region, but General Robert E. Lee settled at White Sulphur Springs in 1867. Lee's residence there brought business, and by the time he died in 1870 The Old White had regained its popularity.

The Chesapeake and Ohio Railroad extended a line to the hotel in 1868, and in 1910 it bought the hotel and its 7,000 acres. Mineral baths, swimming pools, tennis courts, and a nine-hole golf course (later expanded to eighteen holes) were added.

In 1913 the first unit of the present-day Greenbrier was built. Frederick Janius Sterner designed the 250-bedroom, fireproof, Georgian-style mansion to adjoin The Old White. In 1922 The Old White could not pass the fire test, and so was torn down. By the start of World War II, The Greenbrier complex included new wings, a school, and even an airport.

During the war the hotel was used as an internment center for German and Japanese diplomats. In 1942, the federal government acquired the hotel for use as an army hospital, the Ashford General. In 1946, the Chesapeake and Ohio bought back the hotel, extensively remodeled it, and reopened it with a postwar celebratory spirit in 1948. (It is still in the same hands, though the railroad is now part of a vast transportation conglomerate called Chessie System.)

From 1955 until the present, The Greenbrier has continually improved and added to its facilities. Among the many new features are a gun club, theater, auditorium, outdoor pool, bowling lanes, three new eighteen-hole golf courses, a clinic, and new bedroom wings.

The buildings of The Greenbrier complex alone occupy about 25 acres; the entire wooded estate covers 6,500 acres. The main building of the hotel is F. J. Sterner's classical Georgian creation; other buildings are more than 150 years old, and some date from as recent as 1974. Withal, the marriage of traditional and modern styles has been accomplished with taste and elegance.

The Old White is gone, but The Greenbrier, which stands in its place today, is a truly Grand Hotel. And the famous spring that gave birth to the resort still runs in front of the President's Cottage.

Facing page, the entrance to The Greenbrier is framed by towering trees.

Above, the back facade of the hotel, seen from the gardens, has the look of a pre-Civil War plantation.

Left, from yet another view, The Greenbrier presents a gleaming white and beautiful prospect.

Facing page, the 6,500-acre grounds of the hotel provide guests with a variety of settings in which to relax. Here a footpath through a wooded glade offers an inviting route for a stroll.

The elegantly manicured grounds immediately surrounding The Greenbrier contrast with more distant groves of native trees. Pictured *above,* a formal garden with its peaceful symmetry, and *below left,* a fountain framed with trees and shrubbery.

Right, the dining room at The Greenbrier has a summer-house quality about it with its treillage and willow chairs. The fluted columns support brass carriage lanterns.

Left, one of the fireplaces at The Greenbrier, an example of the intricate detail and craftsmanship that can be seen throughout the hotel.

Below, floor-to-ceiling windows and lush potted plants bring the outdoors inside this sun-filled and spacious public room.

The Homestead

HOT SPRINGS, VIRGINIA

The Homestead in Hot Springs, Virginia, can well be described as a reflection of Colonial splendor. Set high in the western Allegheny Mountains on a 16,000-acre site eighty miles from Roanoke, and to the east of The Greenbrier and White Sulphur Springs, The Homestead is the oldest resort in the United States. It is rich in history as well as natural beauty.

According to local accounts, the mineral spring that served as the magnet drawing people to the area was discovered in the Sixteenth Century by an Indian scout traveling to a tribal council. He told his people about the healing waters and soon the hot springs became a neutral region visited by many tribes. Word of the springs spread among the white settlers in the area, but they could not locate them nor could Colonial Governor Spotswood's famous Knights of the Horseshoe. The first recorded discovery by a white man was made by Dr. Thomas Walter, a medical missionary, who wrote about a visit there in 1750: "We went to Hot Springs and found six invalids there. The spring is very clear and warmer than new milk, and there is a spring of cold water within twenty feet of the warm one."

The direct descendant of The Homestead was a simple country inn built by Lieutenant Thomas Bullit, a hero of the Revolutionary War. Bullit had lived in the area for about ten years before America's secession from England, and he returned there at war's end. Unfortunately, he had many visitors who stayed in his home and consumed his supplies while taking the waters. The poor soldier was overwhelmed, and he built the inn in self-defense.

In 1832, Dr. Thomas Goode acquired control of the property and, with heavy advertising, made The Homestead a popular resort and spa that attracted travelers from as far away as Philadelphia. He rebuilt the entire facility in 1846, and by mid-century as many as 15,000 visitors came every year. Upon Dr. Goode's death in 1858, the inn changed hands several times, yet the prestige of the springs increased. During the Civil War, the inn served as a hospital for Confederate soldiers.

In 1890, M. E. Ingalls, president of the Chesapeake and Ohio Railroad, purchased the site on his retirement. Two years later, in 1892, the present bathhouse, located to the east of the central installations, was built, and in 1893 the framed lodge was completed. By the turn of the century, Ingalls had made plans to extensively remodel and enlarge the facilities. Unfortunately, a bakery fire in 1901 razed most of the buildings, except for bathhouse and casino. It turned out to be a blessing in disguise; the fire gave Ingalls an opportunity to erect, from the ground up, a modern resort to rival the best in Europe.

The first new building was completed within a year, but it took thirty years to bring The Homestead to its present handsome condition.

The West Wing was begun in 1903 and completed four years later; the East Wing was added in 1913. The Homestead boasts the oldest American golf course in continuous use. Designed in 1892, the course started humbly enough with six holes, the hazards the old stone walls that divided former pastures. In 1923 the course was enlarged to eighteen holes and the renowned Cascades Course completed. The celebrated clock tower, illuminated at night, was finished in 1929.

By the end of the 1930s, the Depression had taken its toll, and there was some question whether the hotel would remain open. To the rescue came World War II, and the internment of 363 Japanese diplomats, consular personnel, newspapermen, and businessmen. The agreement worked out between the United States government and the hotel stipulated that the prisoners' services and food were to be the same as was received by prewar guests. It was hoped that such remarkable treatment of prisoners might spur the Japanese to treat their American prisoners similarly.

Facing page, the classic lines of The Homestead contribute dignity and grandeur to this fine old hotel.

Ionic columns and open archways are featured in the spacious dining room at The Homestead.

Today The Homestead occupies a great semicircle of manicured grounds surrounded by a wild countryside. The hotel's high ceilings and capacious conference rooms offer guests architectural delights rarely seen today. The Commonwealth Room is gloriously wood paneled; the Great Hall is famous for its white Corinthian columns and valanced windows; the Crystal Room is so called for the magnificent turn-of-the-century crystal chandelier that glitters in its center. The windows there are also valanced, and the capitols of the columns are gold-leafed. Equally regal, but with lower ceilings, are the Dominion and Georgian Rooms. All of the rooms are tastefully furnished and beautifully maintained.

In 1959 the resort introduced skiing to the South. Although the weather is sufficiently cold for snow, nature seldom provides it. The introduction of snow guns enabled the resort to provide a year-round schedule. (In previous winters, registration often fell to as low as ten guests.) A 3,200-foot main slope and runoffs were constructed, and an ice-skating rink was built for winter-sports fans.

The Cascades Stream or Cedar Creek is regularly stocked with rainbow trout, and Bath County proclaims itself the Number One deer county in the state. Horseback riding came to the resort in 1918; before that year horses were a necessity, not a leisurely pastime. The region abounds in natural hiking and riding trails.

Located five miles from The Homestead are the Warm Springs pools; the octagonal men's pool dates from 1761; the round ladies' pool was built in 1836. An old, and appreciated, custom at the pools is the floating out of mint juleps on cork trays to the bathers.

Three miles south of The Homestead, adjoining the golf range, is the fifty-room Cascades Inn. Guests at this small century-old resort enjoy the same privileges as those staying at the larger Homestead. The Inn resembles Mount Vernon with its Colonial simplicity in a rustic setting.

A $9-million South Wing with 190 guest rooms and a fifteen-room conference center was opened in 1973. Situated behind the older buildings, the modern style of the South Wing does not detract from the Colonial architectural harmony. To handle all the facilities and guests, the hotel in peak season employs 1,000 people, an average of approximately one staff member for each one and one-half guests.

The Homestead offers luxury unmarred by ostentation. It has guarded its heritage of old-world virtues—afternoon tea is still served, and semiformal wear is *de rigeur* for dinner—and preserved an estate of cascading streams, rolling hills, verdant glades, forest trails, and lush valleys in much the same naturally beautiful form as they existed in at the time of this nation's birth.

Right, gently rolling lawns and clusters of shade trees characterize the landscaping over much of the 17,000 acres on which The Homestead stands. Deeper woods and winter ski runs are within walking distance of the hotel.

Below, The Homestead as arriving guests see it. The spire and clock tower are visible from miles away.

Left, The Homestead's colonnaded porch is a shady place to watch hotel comings and goings, or just to relax.

Below, the indoor pool, a Victorian-Age addition to the hotel.

WHITEFACE INN

Above, an expansive lawn surrounds the tree-framed main lodge of Whiteface Inn. In the background can be seen the forested land that lies beyond the Inn.

Left, log cabins flanking the main building provide guests with a spectacular view of Lake Placid.

THE LAKE PLACID CLUB

Above, the stone and brick facade of the main building of The Lake Placid Club is further enhanced by towering pines.

Facing page, top, the chapel offers Lake Placid Club guests a quiet retreat in a peaceful setting.

Facing page, bottom, the swimming pool is a recent addition to the year-round resort.

WENTWORTH-BY-THE-SEA

Facing page, the entrance to Wentworth-by-the-Sea, a study in Victorian architectural detail.

Left, the view from the dining room at Wentworth-by-the-Sea.

Below, a circular window in one of the towers looks over the hotel gardens and wooded grounds.

THE GREENBRIER

Facing page, The Greenbrier's Greek Revival entrance bespeaks its antebellum elegance.

Above, the handsome arched windows are capped by scroll-topped Ionic columns, which enhance the classical flavor of the building.

Right, this arched doorway, graceful and inviting, leads to two of the many charming and well-appointed public rooms at The Greenbrier.

THE HOMESTEAD

Facing page, top, a handsome red-brick structure of Georgian design, The Homestead nestles in the foothills of the Allegheny Mountains.

Bottom, the long porch at The Homestead is part of what makes it a hotel in the grand manner.

This page, Greek columns, fretwork, and other classical architectural details harmonize with the outdoor pool and patio, more recent additions to The Homestead.

THE
GREAT LAKES

If the decades between 1870 and 1920 were the glory years for Grand Hotels on the Eastern Seaboard—in New England and New York State, in the warmer southern climes and the mountains of Virginia—it was most decidedly not the case in the Midwest. And yet, in many ways, the Great Lakes region had as much wealth as the Eastern part of the country and it certainly needed a cool retreat from the blistering Midwestern summers.

Mackinac Island, at the northern end of Lake Huron, was the perfect site for the much needed resort. It seemed logical that there should be a luxury hotel there to serve the great industrial centers nearby—Chicago, Detroit, Cleveland, and Saint Louis.

In the mid-1800s word of Mackinac's pleasant summer climate reached as far as Mississippi; the wealthy cotton barons began to spend summers on the island and they constructed baronial homes there. The Civil War called a halt to that, and the Southern planters vanished as their money had. They were replaced by fashionables from Chicago who could reach the island easily by boat. Summer houses and handsome cottages sprang up on acreage overlooking the lake.

In 1881, when ferry service was established, linking the island to the railroads across the strait, Mackinac was really discovered. Six years later ground was broken for the Grand Hotel.

I can still remember my first visit there when I was eleven years old. I was stunned by the size of the Hotel and amazed that there were no cars on the island. Today, many years later, the Grand Hotel is still a stunning sight; and, yes, there are still no cars on the island. Certainly a miracle in these times.

Grand Hotel
MACKINAC ISLAND, MICHIGAN

Often referred to by residents of Mackinac Island as the Mansion on the Hill, the Grand Hotel, the largest summer hotel in the world, is a dazzling sight with its great expanse of white pillars and a porch that extends 880 feet. A favorite vacation spot among Midwesterners, Mackinac Island today looks much the same as it did almost a hundred years ago, when the Grand Hotel opened in 1887. The island itself, three miles long and two miles wide, is beautifully situated, rising majestically above the waters of Lake Huron. The steep cliffs and wooded bluffs provide a handsome setting for the Hotel.

Even before the Civil War, Mackinac Island was a retreat for the wealthy and the elite. When the colossal Hotel was built, it immediately became (and remains today) the greatest tourist attraction in the Great Lakes region. The opening brought national acclaim, and the list of notables who have stayed there runs from movie stars to presidents. Spanning 500 acres from lake shore to bluffs, the Hotel is the island, and the island is the Hotel.

For many years the Grand Hotel operated for only two months of the year—July and August. That it survived at all speaks well for its virtues. For the last twenty-five years, the length of the season has been doubled.

The Hotel had its beginnings in 1882, when Michigan's United States Senator Francis B. Stockbridge visited the island and was so impressed that he decided that a great summer hotel should be built there. The island was a natural paradise, and although there were already hotels there, the Senator envisioned a truly splendid hotel, the most splendid hotel of all—the Grand Hotel.

In 1886, he induced the three transportation companies that served the island, the Michigan Central Railroad, Grand Rapids and Indiana Railroad, and the Detroit and Cleveland Navigation Company, to form the Mackinac Island Hotel Company and purchase the site he had staked out. Construction was begun in 1886 and completed July 10, 1887. The architect was Alphonzo F. Howe; the contractor, Charles W. Caskey.

A wooden structure designed in the Neoclassical style, the Hotel was originally half its present size. The dining room was two stories high in the Hotel's early days but was later remodeled to one story. The facade and porch were lengthened—the porch is said to be the longest at any hotel in the world—and many more rooms were added, including a West Wing. Today, the Hotel is still undergoing improvement and expansion. A golf course and beautifully landscaped grounds are among the many attractions. Horse-drawn carriages are available for on-island transportation, and boating in Lake Huron and, on the western side of the Straits of Mackinac, in Lake Michigan is a popular pastime.

In 1890, after three two-month seasons, the Hotel found itself in financial difficulty. It was leased for ten years to John Hays, at the time Michigan's most prominent hotel operator. Mr. Hays valiantly kept the Hotel open during the Depression of the 1890s and, miraculously, escaped bankruptcy. In 1900, however, after Hays' lease expired, a new manager was found: Henry Weaver, owner of the famous Planters Hotel in Saint Louis.

Mr. Weaver assumed a new ten-year lease, but by 1905 he too was in trouble and informed the transportation combine that owned the hotel that he would have to close at the end of that season. This panicked the transportation people. In an effort to keep the Hotel open for the remaining five years of the lease, they offered Weaver fifty percent of the stock. He also requested, and eventually got, the rest of the stock at the end of the five years. In 1910, nonetheless, Weaver, now full owner of the Hotel, decided to have it razed and the site sold.

Facing page, perched atop a hill, the Grand Hotel overlooks the rest of Mackinac Island and Lake Huron beyond.

This announcement shocked the residents and owners of summer cottages on the island, the economy of which depended on the Hotel. To salvage the resort, Mr. Frank Nagel of Saint Louis and a new group of stockholders bought the Hotel from Weaver.

Thus began several decades of financial ups and downs and changes in management. The two-, and later four-month season undoubtedly has been a major factor in the Grand's struggle to survive. The Great Depression did not help much either. Through it all, guests have flocked to the Hotel and have returned summer after summer to enjoy the luxury of island living, if only for a brief time.

Without a doubt the Grand Hotel is a memorable institution. It is heartening to see it standing today, a magnificent monument to American free enterprise.

This page, guests pause for a shady rest and refreshment at the Golf House on this corner of the Hotel links.

Facing page, the cool breezes from Lake Huron are among the attractions on Mackinac Island; manicured lawns and lush plantings on the grounds of the Grand Hotel provide an excellent milieu in which to enjoy them.

Opposite, cars have been banned from this island's roadways since its earliest days as a resort. Horse-drawn carriages are thus a necessity as well as a charming reminder of another age.

Below, the colonnaded porch, which extends 880 feet around the Grand Hotel. Here strollers approach the vanishing point of just one segment of the shaded walkway.

THE SOUTH

It was in Saint Augustine that Henry Morrison Flagler started his transformation of Florida's Gold Coast. A partner in John D. Rockefeller's Standard Oil Company, Flagler came to Saint Augustine in the 1880s and immediately saw the possibilities in that place of sunshine and palm trees for a winter wonderland, a playground for wealthy Easterners. The Ponce de Leon and The Alcazar were the two hotels Flagler built in Saint Augustine, but they were only the first of the grand designs that were to come.

Henry Flagler was a man of vision and his vision stretched beyond Saint Augustine along the whole east coast of Florida to Miami. The Flagler name lives on in Florida to commemorate that vision. There is a Flagler County, a town called Flagler Beach, and to the south, in Miami, Flagler Street is one of the major downtown arteries. He organized the Florida East Coast Railway, and having thus established access to this semitropical paradise, he set about building hotels. His crowning achievement was The

Breakers in Palm Beach. Twenty or so miles to the south, The Boca Raton Club vies for its glories. That Grand Hotel was the magnum opus of architect/builder Addison Mizner.

The Florida land boom followed in Flagler's wake, reaching a high point in the Twenties. It was the railroads that brought prosperity. As soon as they reached southern Florida, it was easy to lure people to this haven where there was sunshine in winter instead of snow. Once access was established—and by 1913 Flagler had laid track and instituted rail service clear down to Key West—the Florida climate did the rest. Soon "going South for the winter" became a solid status symbol.

Although there were plentiful resorts along the East Coast and in the Virginias that attracted wealthy families, they could not offer the consistently agreeable winter climate of Florida. Vacationers came by private rail car and by automobile to enjoy the magic of winter turned into summer, and Florida was transformed from a wild swampland to a golden nugget.

It may be difficult to visualize today, but before the railroads pushed through Georgia and into Florida, the region was a vast and barren land. There were beautiful lakes and pine forests, but mostly there were swamps. Still, there was the favorable climate, and if the inland areas were marshlike, who could fault the area its keys, the literally dozens of islands that run along the shore on the seaward side? To be able to swim in the ocean in December seemed like a miracle to anyone who had been but a few days earlier a prisoner in the frozen confines of a Northern city like New York or Chicago. If it was impossible to go to the Riviera in France, and it usually was, and if one was seeking the Mediterranean ambience that was then much in vogue, Florida was the answer.

Florida's East Coast boasts the Atlantic Ocean and a splendid tropical climate, but the Southern United States offers also the warm waters of the Gulf of Mexico. There, on a promontory in Mobile Bay, stands The Grand Hotel.

When it was first built, no railroad served the wooden structure; guests arrived by ferry from New Orleans and Mobile. The boats ran on schedule for the wealthy owners of summer homes that stretched for miles along the Gulf, and for the patrons of The Grand Hotel.

Back on the Atlantic Coast, what looks like broken bits of shoreline seaward of Georgia are in fact the breeze-blessed Sea Islands. Far enough south to offer refuge from the icy Northern winter, and separated from the blistering coastal plain by a ribbon of ocean water, the islands are a natural resort location. The Cloister was one of the earliest and certainly the grandest of the hostelries in this now-burgeoning vacation spot.

The Boca Raton Hotel and Club

BOCA RATON, FLORIDA

Located on Florida's Gold Coast, the town of Boca Raton has all the resources required of a seaside resort—the average year-round temperature is seventy-two degrees, the pleasant subtropical climate is warmed in winter by the Gulf Stream and cooled in summer by trade winds. The Boca Raton Hotel, which is the town's greatest glory, is the fruit of the imagination of architect Addison Mizner.

Mizner is said to have been the creator of Florida's unique architectural style and the man who transformed Palm Beach into the social center of its day. With the help of his brother Wilson, he set out to do the same for Boca Raton and his plans were ambitious indeed. The two brothers originally envisioned a $100-million development at Boca Raton, including the world's largest ocean-front hotel, the small Cloister Inn overlooking a man-made lake, and twenty miles of Venetian-style canals bordered by home sites (each costing $20,000). Addison also intended to build for himself a million-dollar castle, complete with drawbridge, in the middle of the dredged lagoon, now called Lake Boca Raton. He envisioned turning the 17,500-acre site into "a happy combination of Venice and Heaven, Florence and Toledo, with a little Greco-Roman glory and grandeur thrown in." What he came up with was the $1.5-million "small" Cloister Inn, perhaps the most expensive 100-room hotel ever built. It remains today as the heart of a sprawling and soaring resort complex.

Mizner's jewel of a hotel boasted priceless antiques, fountains, tiled patios, and arched windows. Every room looked out onto gardens, fountains, and palm trees. This open, airy design is central to Mizner's philosophy. There is a Spanish feeling to the place, but with a difference: There are courts and corridors, balconies and balustrades, high windows, galleries, and exterior stairways, but all are removed from the confines of a central courtyard. "What I really did," Mizner explained, "was turn the Spanish inside out like a glove, making all the openings face a patio or courtyard. I made every room face two or three ways."

The Mizners spared no expense in pursuing their palatial fantasy. They strove for authenticity, or the look of it. What could be imported was; what could not was created especially for their needs. Faced with Florida's lack of native stone, they developed a casting works to imitate limestone, granite, and marble. Afterward the fake stone was machine tooled to give the effect of hand-cutting. Addison had the red roofing tiles custom made at his factory in West Palm Beach.

Lobby and halls are resplendent with antiques brought mainly from Central America and Spain. There are a number of fine dark wood pieces, such as the great refectory table that stands at the west end of the lobby, a massive Seventeenth-Century credenza with a gold-embossed mirror, an Italian vestry settee, and several handsome writing desks. Many of the antiques, it was found, could not withstand the summer rains: iron nails rusted, leather mildewed, veneer came unglued. To deal with those hazards Mizner opened his own wood-carving works; he imported the finest walnut logs and pegged and joined the wood for durability. He also opened a forge to make lamps, candlesticks, and railings.

The Cloister Inn opened in February 1926 under Ritz-Carlton management. Guests included such notables as actress Marie Dressler, Princess Chika of Romania, Irving Berlin, Lady Diana Manners, General T. Coleman du Pont, and the Wall Street tycoon Jesse L. Livermore. It was a glorious season, but a brief one. By April 1926, the hotel closed. It next fell into the hands of former United States Vice-President Charles G. Dawes, who ran it sporadically until 1928, when Clarence H. Geist, a Philadelphia utilities magnate, purchased

Facing page, The Boca Raton Hotel stands like a Spanish castle against the Florida sky. The arches, arabesques, and turrets of the original structure are echoed by the detailing in the tower addition.

the Inn and its furnishings, the golf courses, tennis courts, and bathing beach for $1 million. Mr. Geist wanted to make the Inn the most noteworthy private club in the world, catering to the heads of American finance, captains of industry, statesmen, and the first families of America. He acquired other holdings in the vicinity, including 112 acres of oceanfront for a casino and air field.

Geist spent $8 million developing the surrounding 2,000 acres and constructing a $3.5-million hotel, which was attached to The Cloister Inn. Architects were Schultze and Weaver of New York, the same firm that designed The Breakers Hotel in Palm Beach. When construction was finished, The Boca Raton Hotel and Club consisted of 400 bedrooms, five patios (including the luxurious Patio Royale, made from the lobby of the original Cloister Inn structure), a wide rocking-chair terrace, two swimming pools, a sanitorium, a special dining room for children and another for the maids and chauffeurs of guests, quarters for the army of employees, and space for stores and shops. Mr. Geist imported a French landscape gardener to beautify the grounds, and he purchased the entire stock of one plant nursery to embellish the patios. The large colonnaded Garden Pool was designed in the style of ancient Roman baths.

At the east end of the Patio Royale, which had been an open area in Mizner's plan but was enclosed as part of the remodelling, the open Dining Colonnade was built. It is itself enclosed today—such are the requirements of air-conditioned comfort—but its fine Renaissance-style columns remain. Construction on the beach included The Cabana Club, a large double curve of cabanas each equipped with sitting and dressing rooms, showers, and a canopied porch. Mr. Geist also opened a channel from Lake Boca Raton to the beach, cleared the lake of the island upon which Mizner had planned to build his castle, and dredged the lake bottom to uniform depth. He next had the Boca Raton inlet dredged and built 400-foot concrete and stone jetties to permit yachts to tie up.

The new Club opened in 1930; membership requirements included the purchase of $5,000 worth of stock in the Spanish River Land Firm and dues of $100 a year. Geist personally met the yearly deficits, and he ran the Club in a despotic fashion until his death at seventy-three in 1938. In his will, he left the Club an annual subsidy of $100,000 for five years.

Despite the fact that it opened in the midst of the Great Depression, The Boca Raton Club managed to attract the wealthy and the powerful whose fortunes had not been decimated by the country's financial agonies. Visiting dignitaries included President Hoover, several du Ponts, and Edward Stettinius, then Secretary of State. The press and public were completely barred, affording guests seclusion and surcease from a depressed America.

The Boca Raton Club was taken over by the United States Army in 1942 to house trainées. Bunks and Government Issue furniture replaced the luxurious decor, and the facilities were referred to as "the most elegant barracks in history."

The Boca Raton's modern era began in 1956, when aluminum pioneer Arthur Vining Davis purchased the resort plus 1,000 acres of surrounding land and a mile of oceanfront property for $22.5 million. Mr. Davis subsequently organized the Arvida Corporation, and in 1958 his new corporation took possession of the hotel facilities. A $20-million program of extensive refurbishing and construction was begun in 1969, which added a twenty-seven-story tower of guest rooms and a new convention center. During the expansion, the garden swimming pool was relocated, and that site became The Camino Room, an exhibition center. The expansion added 257 sleeping rooms and suites.

Much has changed at The Boca Raton Hotel and Club since Addison Mizner began dreaming about a little bit of Venice and a little bit of Heaven. The Cloister, the one structure he did complete, remains as the focal point of the extensive buildings and property. And the Hotel is now one of the South's leading luxury resorts.

Facing page, an avenue of Royal palms leads to the entrance of The Boca Raton Hotel and Club.

This page, above, the twenty-seven-story tower was added at the end of the Sixties to expand Hotel facilities. Its tasteful design harmonizes with the older buildings surrounding it.

Left, the side foyer of The Boca Raton Hotel. Addison Mizner's design included the ironwork balcony and Moorish arches shown here.

Facing page, The Boca Raton Hotel is Mizner's fantasy come to life: "A happy combination of Venice and Heaven, Florence and Toledo, with a little Greco-Roman glory and grandeur thrown in."

The Breakers

PALM BEACH, FLORIDA

The Breakers in Palm Beach rises like a giant monolith against an azure blue sky and beside bluer waters. The architecture is magnificent, the white granite walls sparkle in the sun and reflect moonlight at night. The sweeping facade and the Florentine fountain at the entrance charm visitors. Although The Breakers has always been renowned for its opulence, for years it had to compete with the neighboring Royal Poinciana, then the largest resort hotel in the world. But a hurricane in 1934 ended the rivalry and the aristocratic Breakers towers alone above Palm Beach.

It was Henry Flagler who was responsible for both Palm Beach and The Breakers. He had made his fortune in a partnership with John D. Rockefeller, was able to retire at fifty-three, and came to Florida in 1883 to relax.

Mesmerized by the climate and unspoiled beauty of the state, he began construction two years later on The Ponce de Leon Hotel in Saint Augustine, then a historic, but sleepy outpost. Flagler intended his hotel to cater to the wealthy for the winter season. Realizing, however, that poor transportation hampered hotel business, he started buying out the local railroads and soon became the largest railroad controller in the state. With good rail access, The Breakers became a success almost overnight, and Saint Augustine's popularity as a resort community was secure. To meet the increased demand Flagler built a second hotel in Saint Augustine, The Alcazar.

Ten years after he came to Florida, Flagler discovered Lake Worth about 250 miles to the south of Saint Augustine. Actually, it is not a lake but a wide channel between the mainland and a chain of tidal islands. Jupiter was the only town in the region and it was serviced by the Celestial Railroad Company, so named because it linked the communities of Jupiter, Mars, Venus, and Juno. Flagler was intrigued with one island in particular; it was covered with palm trees and lay on the east side of the lake. He learned that years before a Spanish ship, the *Providencia,* had been wrecked nearby and its cargo of coconuts washed ashore. Pioneer settlers had planted the coconuts, hoping to harvest copra. If the copra did not flourish, the palm trees themselves did, almost to the point of taking over the island.

Flagler was enchanted by the beauty of the place as well as by the translucent blue of the Atlantic Ocean there, and he decided to acquire the property for a resort community. The problems of construction were monumental and the price of the land skyrocketed as soon as the owners learned of his plans, but Flagler, undaunted, started ground-breaking in May 1893 and within nine months The Royal Poinciana Hotel was opened.

Flagler preserved a section of the island for the Hotel grounds, and his resort community, renamed Palm Beach, met with immediate success. Its popularity was so great, in fact, that Flagler decided to build a second hotel on the far side of his island. The ninety-room Palm Beach Inn was the first of three hotels to be built on the site of The Breakers. Flagler had also established a steamship line running between Palm Beach and Nassau in the Bahamas, and a pier was constructed so that his steamers could dock near the main entrance.

In 1905, the Inn, which had been renamed The Breakers, burned down. Within a year another Breakers took its place, this time with 250 rooms. In 1925, the structure burned again, and the Flagler family made plans to rebuild the present structure: a massive, fireproof building with classically ornate rooms. The purpose was "luxurious comfort in an atmosphere of refined exclusiveness."

The new Breakers was built in the record time of less than a year, ready for a 1926 opening. The architecture was reminiscent of the Villa Medici in Rome with its twin towers

Facing page, the imposing front entrance of The Breakers is a study in contrast. The simple lines of the massive edifice are softened by the lightness and grace of the fountain that stands before it.

This page, glittering crystal chandeliers, stately columns, the rib-vaulted ceiling, and flawless marble floor are reminiscent of a Renaissance *palazzo.*

Facing page, this groin-vaulted outdoor passageway is a prime example of the sort of architectural detail that makes The Breakers so impressive.

and graceful arches. The fountain showcased in front of the hotel is patterned after one in the Boboli Gardens of Florence. The Breakers, which cost $6 million to build, is still considered one of the most imposing hotels in the world.

The Italian Renaissance structure is situated on a 200-acre site and looks the same today as it did on its opening day a half century ago. A stroll through the hotel is like a one-day tour of the great Renaissance *palazzi* of Italy. Genoa's Palazzo Carega appears to have been transplanted to Palm Beach with its vast corridor lobby graced by frescoes and vaulted ceilings. The lobby overlooks a central courtyard, reminiscent of the inner gardens of Villa Sante in Rome. East of the courtyard is the Mediterranean Ballroom, inspired by the Palazzo Imperiale in Genoa.

The Palazzo Ducale of Venice is recreated on the ceiling of the Gold Room. A series of portraits surrounding the upper wall of the room depict Europeans who participated in the discovery of America; the overpanel of the great stone fireplace shows the earth turning on its axis until the old world meets the new. Spectacular paintings, chandeliers, and ormolu detailing decorate the beamed ceilings of the dining rooms, one of which is modeled after that in the Florentine Palazzo Davanzati; another is painted with scenes of Italian cities and regions. A huge Venetian chandelier of bronze, mirrors, and crystal hangs from the center of the circular skylight.

In 1969 the hotel expanded, adding the elegant Venetian Ballroom that overlooks the ocean, The Alcazar Lounge, and the new South Wing. The Alcazar Lounge, Moorish in design, was named after Flagler's old Alcazar Hotel in Saint Augustine.

Today, The Breakers includes 600 rooms and suites, all with views of beach or gardens. Guests have at their disposal two swimming pools (one salt water outdoors, the other fresh water indoors), protected ocean swimming from the private beach, twelve tennis courts, and a children's playground.

The Breakers combines the best of the old and the finest of the new. From its columned porte-cochere to its vast corridor lobby, and from the turquoise waters to the white sandy beach, The Breakers is a rewarding experience for the selective traveler.

Above, a courtyard garden at The Breakers.

Below, gracefully curving arches and tiled roofs mark the entrance to the hotel. Twin belvedere towers are a fitting cap to the building.

Opposite, a work of art needs no words to describe it; so it is with this frescoed dome ceiling.

Elegance is the watchword in this lobby, as it is throughout The Breakers.

GRAND HOTEL

Left, seen from a distance, the Grand Hotel on Mackinac Island sings of bygone days. Its 880-foot colonnaded porch is said to be the world's longest.

Below, horse-drawn carriages are among the old-world delights of the Grand Hotel. Since no automobiles are allowed on Mackinac Island, they are also the principal mode of transport.

THE BOCA RATON HOTEL AND CLUB

Facing page, the mingling of old and new: Addison Mizner's brilliant interpretation of Spanish architectural styles stretches out below the twenty-seven-story tower, which was added to The Boca Raton Club in 1967.

Right, the pink stucco and red-tile roofed Boca Raton Club sits like a jewel in a verdant setting.

Below, quiet elegance is reflected in the interior of the Hotel. Note the handsome coffered ceiling and sweeping staircase.

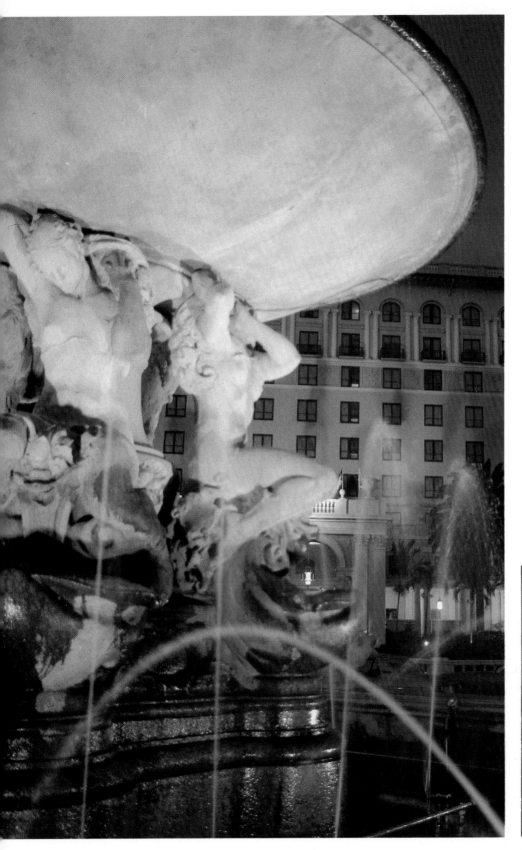

THE BREAKERS

Facing page, top, the grandeur of another era is recalled by the entrance of The Breakers.

Facing page, bottom, the lobby of The Breakers is an architectural wonder: splendid vaulted ceilings and glistening marble floors frame its great expanse. The elegant tracery of exotic fishtail palms completes the scene.

This page, left, aglow in the night, the magnificent carved stone fountain can be seen against the background of the hotel entrance.

This page, below, a closeup of one of the extraordinary ceilings at The Breakers.

101

THE GRAND HOTEL

Top, The Grand Hotel in Point Clear, Alabama, offers a quiet retreat. The main building, with its handsome gambrel roof, faces Mobile Bay and affords guests a splendid view as well as cooling breezes.

Bottom, trees and flowers flourish in the semitropical climate of this Gulf Coast resort. The plantings on the grounds are designed to create a cool and shady ambience.

THE CLOISTER

Facing page, at The Cloister, serenity can be found in the low profile of the buildings and the lushly landscaped grounds.

Above, these arched and leaded church windows form a lovely background to the colorful flower beds.

Right, the enclosed porch area has a distinctly European flavor.

The Grand Hotel

POINT CLEAR, ALABAMA

Point Clear, Alabama, is an unspoiled area where prevailing breezes from the Gulf of Mexico make hot summer days comfortable and winter days mild.

Located on the eastern shore of Mobile Bay, it is a lovely place of blue-green waters and sloping white-sand beaches. The Bay itself is one of the great natural harbors in the United States, stretching eight to eighteen miles wide, meeting the Gulf of Mexico between Florida and Mississippi.

The site on which The Grand Hotel sits today has seen two earlier hotels so named; and the area surrounding the hotel and grounds has had a long and exciting (at times tragic) history. It begins in 1847, when a Mr. Chamberlain built a rambling, 100-foot long, two-story hotel with lumber brought down from Mobile by sailboats. There were forty guest rooms and a shaded front gallery with outside stairs at each end. The dining room was located in an adjacent structure, and a third two-story building, called The Texas, housed the bar. Destroyed in an 1893 hurricane, the bar was rebuilt and, according to one contemporary report, "It was the gathering place for the merchants of the South, and poker games with high stakes, and billiards enlivened with the best of liquors were their pastimes."

A fourth building, a two-story frame mansion called Gunnison House, was originally a private summer residence. It became a popular meeting place before the Civil War. Cognac flowed freely, gambling money changed hands fast, and the feasts were sumptuous. A headquarters during the war for Confederate blockade-runners, the structure today bears the scars of battle. A gaping hole marks the entry point of a cannonball fired during the Battle of Mobile Bay, and The Grand Hotel has the distinction of being the only North American resort ever to have been involved in a battle.

During the war, the Hotel and Gunnison House were used as army hospitals. Other buildings housed officers, and, in the war's final days, the Twenty-first Alabama Regiment camped on the east grounds.

The Hotel reopened after the war, but was almost totally destroyed by a fire in 1869. Miraculously, none of the 150 guests was injured, and all their personal effects, as well as the Hotel linens and most of the furniture, were saved.

Repairs were made and the Hotel was soon again enjoying a prosperous existence. But then, in August 1871, tragedy struck. The twenty-seven-ton steamer *Ocean Wave* exploded at the Point Clear pier and scores of Hotel guests died. For years afterward sections of the wrecked steamer could be spotted during low tide.

After the explosion, Captain H. C. Baldwin of Mobile acquired the property, and at a cost of $75,000 built a new hotel that resembled the earlier 100-foot-long structure, but was three times as long! Baldwin's son-in-law, George Johnson, Louisiana State Treasurer, took an active role in the business and assumed charge upon Baldwin's death. This two-story facility of sixty suites was opened in 1875. That summer the Hotel was filled to capacity. Steamers stopped at Point Clear three times a week bringing Hotel guests; by 1889 boats arrived daily. The winter rates were two dollars a day, ten dollars weekly, and forty dollars by the month. The resort flourished.

In the 1890s, Point Clear was the center of the most brilliant social life in the Deep South. Boats crowded with pleasure-seekers from Mobile and New Orleans docked at the pier; carriages and tandem bikes dashed in and out of the drive; blaring bands and picnickers flocked to the broad lawns. Point Clear with its Grand Hotel was known as "The Queen of Southern Resorts."

By 1939, however, the place was so badly rundown that its new owners, the Waterman Steamship Company, had it razed and, in 1940, built Grand Hotel III. This was a modern air-conditioned building with ninety rooms; it spread long and low, with giant picture

The lobby of The Grand Hotel is characterized by a handsome blend of wood and stone. Note the beamed cathedral ceiling.

windows and glassed-in porches. A few years later cottages were constructed, utilizing lumber, especially the fine heart-pine flooring and framing, from the old building. During World War II, when the shipping company turned over the facilities to the United States government for $1 million, it was with the stipulation that the soldiers were not to wear shoes indoors lest they damage the pine floors.

In 1955 the Hotel was acquired by McLean Industries, and ten years later J. K. McLean himself bought it and formed the present Grand Hotel Company. A new fifty-room addition was built, and extensive improvements were made.

Today the four-season Grand Hotel stands on the sharp triangle of the Point, the property extending back for several hundred acres. The oldest hotel on the Gulf Coast, it consists of a central three-story building flanked by four two-story wings. Guest cottages have a view of Mobile Bay as well as excellent exposure to breeze and sun. Almost all of the 122 guest rooms and suites, in the main Hotel and in the cottages, are distinguished by lustrous golden-brown paneling from local cypress trees. The massive dining room ceiling was made from ship timbers, and huge picture windows on three sides of the room offer marvelous views of the Bay.

The Grand Hotel boasts one of the best golf courses in the South: 6,713 yards from long tees, with a par 70. Fish River, where speckled trout and bass are caught, is eight miles northeast of the resort, and deep-sea fishing is available on the resort's own power cruisers. Cottages extend along one side of the Point up to the yacht harbor and small boat anchorage. On the other side of the Point is probably the largest swimming pool maintained by a private resort: It is 140 feet wide, bordered by paved terraces and roofed shelters, and faced by a picturesque lagoon that is fed by a fountain. There are also ten tennis courts, beach swimming, winter skiing, sailing, horseback riding, skeet and trap shooting, and cycling.

Facing page, the lobby and reception area viewed from the railed balcony above.

This page, lush green shrubbery and shade trees festooned with Spanish moss lend a cool and peaceful air to this Gulf Coast resort.

The Cloister

SEA ISLAND, GEORGIA

Set on a tropical island resplendent with magnolias, cypress groves, and open salt marshes, The Cloister of Sea Island, Georgia, is a sophisticated yet informal family resort. It was built in 1928, at a time when the focus was on Florida, its neighbor to the South. All the same, the new sixty-nine-room hotel was an immediate success.

Sea Island is one of the Golden Isles of Georgia. Inhabited by wealthy plantation owners, the islands did not immediately suggest themselves as a fashionable tourist mecca. Indeed, the privileged islanders fled the region during the hot summers, heading either to the mountains inland or to Europe. The success of the tourist industry on the islands in the Twentieth Century was due to the increased use of the automobile, better highways, air conditioning, and the popularity of boating.

In 1911, an automotive engineer named Howard E. Coffin came to Savannah, Georgia, to take part in the Vanderbilt Cup Races. During the visit, he was treated to a hunting and fishing party on Sapelo Island, which is north of the Sea Island group. Intrigued by the natural beauty of the place, he began acquiring island property; eventually he developed a plantation and shooting reserve and rebuilt an historic mansion there for use as a vacation home. During the next decade, on one of his trips to Georgia, Coffin learned that the state was planning to build a causeway from the main North-South coastal road at Brunswick, to link the mainland with Saint Simons Island, directly west of Sea Island. Realizing that property values would soon skyrocket, Coffin began purchasing land on Saint Simons.

In surveying the area for further purchases, Coffin discovered Sea Island, one of the smallest in the Golden Isles group. It is separated from its larger neighbors by narrow channels of the Black Banks River and Village Creek. Here Coffin saw ancient semitropical trees, gigantic oaks garlanded with Spanish moss, towering pines, fragrant gardens of magnolias and juniper, magnificent ocean beaches, and rolling dunes. He purchased the land forthwith, intending to build a vast family resort to be surrounded with residential cottages. The plans called for an ornate complex in a Spanish architectural style, with indoor and outdoor pools, sunken gardens, fountains, and every conceivable elegance. These original ideas were not carried out; a smaller, simpler, though nonetheless elegant hotel was planned for the southern end of the island. Addison Mizner was hired as architect.

Mizner was the creator of the fabulous Boca Raton Hotel and Club. This eccentric genius, whose flair for extravagance sent him into bankruptcy in building his Florida resort, resurrected the name—The Cloister—but set his sights at a more modest level. His Georgia hotel was a forty-six-room, Mediterranean-style building. The red tile roofs, the low profile, and the mixture of architectural elements are reminiscent of the original Cloister at Boca Raton, yet the Sea Island Cloister is a unique and quietly elegant resort.

Since its opening in 1928, the original building has been enlarged and modified. There are now more than 264 guest rooms in the hotel and more than 325 cottages in the island's central section. The original 6,000 acres of property has been expanded to 12,000 acres. All structures are still low-rise, none exceeding three stories, to keep them below the tree-line, and the Mediterranean style prevails.

The five-mile beach is one of the longest and finest on the Eastern Seaboard, reaching to the Black Banks River. The main hotel is set back several hundred yards from the beach. The terraces of River House overlook the river and the extraordinary marshes beyond; the Beach Houses face the sea, each room with a view of the ocean. Guest cottages are adjacent to the beach houses. Red and white magnolia blossoms provide a splendid background for the sun-splashed walls, red-tiled roofs, and brick chimneys of the resort buildings.

Facing page, a view of the sun-splashed Cloister garden from a cool and shady interior.

Facing page, Mediterranean tile roofs top the glistening stucco walls of this jewel box of a hotel.

This page, right, the low buildings of The Cloister, screened by palms and climbing greenery, create a scene of immense charm.

Below, the lobby at The Cloister is beautifully appointed. Note the timbered ceiling and the cinquefoil arch windows.

ARIZONA AND COLORADO

By the early 1900s the Eastern Seaboard was dotted with several large resort hotels, grand in style and with more than enough guests to fill them. The wealthy of the Northeast and South comprised a social class that demanded resort vacations. The luxurious havens they frequented were generally developed in scenic areas where either sea breezes or healing waters were strong attractions. In California, not yet heavily populated, a few grand resorts had been built. They were called spas, or simply "the place to go" if you had money. But what about the vast acreage in between? Colorado, for example? This too was a scenic area with glorious mountains and fine clean air. Why not a resort there?

The tiny settlement of Colorado Springs, 5,000 feet above sea level and only ten miles from Pike's Peak, was founded in 1871, and climate was its claim to fame. There, in pure mountain air, one could find relief from asthma or recover from tuberculosis. The place was famous far and wide for its fresh-air cures. The socially prominent of England flocked to Rocky Mountain resorts as much for status as for the cure, in much the same manner as Americans traveled to European spas. In fact, so many wealthy English people visited Colorado Springs that for a time it was known as "Little London."

Colorado is also Mother Lode Country —there was gold in those mountains and prospectors came to find it. Those who did get rich made the town prosperous. Indeed, it was a mining fortune that built the fashionable Broadmoor.

It was a good many years later, in the 1920s, that the hot, dry desert air came to be considered a health bonus as well. Until that time, the cities of the Southwest, Phoenix in particular, were barren outposts. Today, Phoenix is one of this country's fastest growing metropolitan centers, but in the early years of this century it took farsighted vision to imagine that a Grand Hotel might flourish in that arid landscape. But farsighted it was, and the result, the Arizona Biltmore, is a showplace of a hotel and a genuine American treasure.

The Broadmoor

COLORADO SPRINGS, COLORADO

The Broadmoor, set on the rim of Broadmoor Lake, has been called the Riviera of the Rockies. Although four miles from downtown Colorado Springs at the edge of Cheyenne Mountain, it has an unmistakably Mediterranean air about it. Many of the decorations of the pink stucco and red tile roofed structure were brought from art centers in Europe and other parts of the world to create what is an outstanding resort.

Like so many of America's great hotels, the present Broadmoor structure is not the original—far from it. The first hotel on the spot was built between 1896 and 1897. It was a simple, three-story, Colonial-style building which accommodated 135 guests. But if the building was simple, the story behind it most decidedly is not. It was one of two buildings constructed by Count James Pourtales of Silesia, which was then a part of Germany. How this unlikely figure arrived on the Colorado scene follows:

The Count had come to America hoping to get rich quick. He needed funds to restore *Glumbowitz*, his mountain estate. To this end, he formed a land and investment corporation, bought the Colorado Springs site on which The Broadmoor now stands, and plotted and divided tracts on a 2,400-acre area. As an enticement to developers, he promised to build a casino that would rival any European pleasure palace. In addition, the Count laid out streets, landscaped and irrigated the property, and built an artificial lake.

In the end, Pourtales' casino turned out to be Georgian in style, modeled after the Imperial Palace at Potsdam in Germany. The casino was a satisfaction to him and a curiosity for the crowds who came to see this unique white-pillared building. And come they did, until the Depression of 1893. Although the casino did not close, the Pourtales' holdings fell into receivership, and then, in 1897, the nemesis of all wood structures, fire, struck and burned the hotel to the ground. It was quickly replaced by a scaled-down, two-story affair that was later to be moved south and become The Broadmoor Golf Club. The hotel itself closed, then reopened as a girls' school in 1913, and finally, in 1915, it again became a hotel. When the present Broadmoor facilities were opened, the old 1913 structure was converted into The Colonial Club, which was eventually razed when the Broadmoor South addition was built.

At about the same time as the old hotel was reopening, two entrepreneurs named Spencer Penrose and C. M. MacNeill were engaged in negotiations to purchase The Antlers Hotel in downtown Colorado Springs. Noting the beauty of the area and also mindful of the success of Florida and Virginia spas, the two men dreamed of turning the Rocky Mountain town into a fashionable resort area. When they were unable to get the price they wanted, they focused their attention on the Broadmoor site. They were never interested in the old facilities; they wanted to build a large fashionable hotel from the ground up on the land facing Broadmoor Lake.

Rumors abounded when news of Penrose's intentions leaked out. It was said that the million-dollar hotel would be designed by a famous hotel architect and would be four stories high, of white stucco, and situated on the west side of the lake. They were close. Frederick Janius Sterner, designer of The Greenbrier in West Virginia and of The Antlers, was commissioned for the job. Sterner decided to place the hotel on the *east* side of the lake and give it an Italian look. Pink stucco and three forty-foot arches capped by a balustrade were part of the plan. The management, however, declared Sterner's proposal too elaborate, and his contract was terminated.

In November 1916, Warren and Wetmore of New York were given the job. This was the firm responsible for designing Grand Central Station and The Biltmore, Ritz-Carlton,

Vanderbilt, and Belmont Hotels in Manhattan. Their plans were approved in late January 1917, with a projected cost of $650,000, not including service buildings. Bids, however, ranged even higher—from $900,000 to $1,055,000. Finally, James Stewart and Company was awarded the building contract after it promised to finish the hotel in the record time of a year, the war and a manpower and supply shortage notwithstanding. To meet the deadline, 400 to 500 people were employed at one time.

Construction began on May 20, 1917. The building was *not* entirely finished by the informal June 1, 1918 opening date. Hundreds attended the dinner-dance preview, but no overnight guests were permitted. Mr. and Mrs. John D. Rockefeller and party were among those turned away. Their fifth- and sixth-floor suites were not yet ready, so the party was shuttled over to Penrose's competitor, The Antlers. By June 10, however, the guest rooms were completed, and by June 15 a swimming party inaugurated the blue-and-white-tile, heated indoor pool. The total expense of the construction, gala openings, and publicity amounted to an estimated nearly $2 million.

During the 1920s, Penrose and his wife Julie decorated their hotel handsomely with paintings, sculptures, rugs, fixtures, and fine furniture, selected by the couple on their world tours and shipped back to the hotel. These included a Seventeenth-Century painting of Marie Antoinette by the Spanish painter Claudius Coello, which hangs in the mezzanine sunroom and, outside the hotel, a fabulous 200-year-old Venetian fountain featuring mythological horses.

The Broadmoor became a favorite of New York society, and money poured freely into Penrose's coffers. Indeed, the only blot on this dream was Prohibition. But even in that, Penrose was not caught out as badly as many another hotelier. He had been forewarned and had stocked his cellars before the nation went dry. He is reputed to have had the most extensive liquor stash in America during the thirsty decade.

In 1921 the Broadmoor Invitational Golf Tournament was established, and in 1924 a polo field was built. A night club opened in 1928, and in 1929, speculating on a golden future, Penrose constructed a hangar for private planes. And then came the Wall Street Crash.

The Broadmoor was deeply affected by the Depression. Although the Hotel was never in danger of falling out of Penrose's hands (his huge investments held him over), he was forced to take many economy measures. Business declined drastically—the 1930–1931 season was the worst—and Penrose had to reduce the staff; doormen, elevator operators, and bellboys worked for tips only. Within a year, The Colonial Club and the main building were the only facilities open. The four wings were closed, the kitchen staff was down to seven, and at one time during the peak season guests numbered only sixty. Throughout this period the hotel kept alive by catering to local activities, such as supper dances, teas, bridge tournaments, and pet shows. Even so the hotel was forced to close during the winter season of 1935–1936.

By 1937 the situation began to improve; the management renovated thirty-seven guest rooms and made a few other conservative improvements. But it was the best season of the decade, and Penrose, ever optimistic, marked the occasion by dedicating his latest project, the Will Rogers Shrine of the Sun, located on the other side of Cheyenne Mountain. In 1939 The Tavern opened; it was formerly known as The Rendezvous. Lining the corridors was a display of Penrose's collection of over one thousand whiskey and wine bottles, *not one a duplicate.*

Unlike many hotels, The Broadmoor was not taken over by the government to house servicemen during World War II. It continued to function as a private hotel and, except for a temporary drop in attendance when gasoline rationing was imposed, it continued to thrive.

A large expansion and refurbishment program was launched after the war. The

Commanding a view of mountain and water, The Broadmoor sparkles in the afternoon sun.

kitchenette apartments of Northeastmoor and Southeastmoor were constructed, and the outdoor swimming pool was extended into the lake. The entire facility was repainted, new wiring added, and guest rooms were gradually redecorated. In 1960 the rooms were air-conditioned, and the greenhouse was again expanded. In 1961 the old indoor swimming pool was closed, the space converted into a modern drugstore in 1963. The world's largest hyperbolic paraboloid, the International Center, was opened in 1961, and it now features theatrical events as well as conventions. The Broadmoor South was also begun in 1961, adding 145 rooms in nine stories. And in 1976 the Broadmoor West was added, a 156-room expansion directly across Cheyenne Lake from the main hotel on the site of the Spencer Penrose Stadium. This addition is four stories high, and its Italian Renaissance style with pink stucco and red tile roofs blends harmoniously with the older buildings.

Today, The Broadmoor facilities boast 560 rooms in thirty major buildings. And the sleepy Rocky Mountain town of Colorado Springs is a metropolis of over 200,000 people. What began as a bankrupt Silesian Count's fund-raising scheme has become one of America's grandest grand hotels.

This lobby area is exquisitely appointed with fluted columns topped by ornamental urns. The lattice-work plaster ceiling is a crowning touch.

Right, the Golf Club is a treasured reminder of The Broadmoor's early days. Built at the end of the last century, it was at one time the main hotel building.

Below, in contrast, this is one of the newer additions to The Broadmoor complex. Its sleek, uncluttered lines blend well with the older structures.

Arizona Biltmore

PHOENIX, ARIZONA

The Arizona Biltmore seems to rise naturally out of the desert landscape, so harmonious is structure with environment. The hotel stands as a testament to the genius of its guiding spirit, Frank Lloyd Wright.

In 1927 the McArthur family, well established in Phoenix, decided that a luxurious hotel, designed to suit the shining foothills on the north side of the city, was what Phoenix needed. Albert Chase McArthur, himself an architect, called upon Frank Lloyd Wright for help on his project. McArthur had, twenty years before, worked with the eminent architect in his Oak Park, Illinois, office.

The site for the new hotel was by no means spectacular but it had an intangible beauty. Destruction of the landscape was kept to a minimum to preserve a natural environment for a building of handsome design. The hotel is an incredible feat of construction, based on the precast concrete-block system that Frank Lloyd Wright had used previously in some California homes. The blocks are decorated with abstract patterns and in some cases are perforated to develop contrasts of light and shadow. The roof was made from copper mined in Arizona.

The Arizona Biltmore was opened officially on September 23, 1929. Although austere on the exterior, the interior featured many appointments of understated elegance: The lobby glowed with gold-leaf ceiling, columns, and fountains. The carpet in the lobby was from a design that Wright executed in 1917, as were the light fixtures and some of the upholstered furniture. The handsome wrought-iron furniture was made by Warren and Gilbert Chase McArthur in 1928.

Toward the end of 1929, chewing gum magnate William Wrigley, Jr., of Chicago, Illinois, purchased the hotel, along with 1,200 adjacent acres. For forty-four years the Wrigley family owned the hotel and made it the unique luxury feature in the area. The Wrigleys themselves spent a good part of the year in a mansion adjacent to the hotel. In 1973 the family sold the hotel to Talley Industries, which immediately began looking into expansion plans to meet the demands of a swiftly growing population in Phoenix.

A new sprinkler system was being installed in the summer of 1973 when a spark from a welding torch ignited insulation material and a fire roared throughout the roof and crawlspace above the fourth floor. The Phoenix fire department miraculously got the six-alarm fire under control in something over two hours. The hotel had been closed for renovations so no guests were injured, but the copper roof was damaged and many other areas of the hotel required extensive repair. Talley Industries enlisted the professional assistance of the Taliesin Associated Architects and Interior Designers, keepers of the Frank Lloyd Wright legacy. They helped rebuild and refurbish the hotel in record time. Original Frank Lloyd Wright drawings were secured from the Wright Foundation and, in consultation with Mrs. Franz G. Talley, designs were selected for furniture, carpets, fabrics, and murals.

By September 29, 1973, exactly forty-four years from the day the hotel originally opened, repairs and improvements were completed. Like the Phoenix of legend, out of the ashes rose a more complete and beautiful hotel than had existed before the fire.

Facing page, the building Frank Lloyd Wright inspired is angular and imposing, its clean lines and geometric proportions punctuated by subtle detailing.

Facing page, a pillared, sculptural concept predominates in the design of the hotel. The carved and perforated patterns in the cast concrete blocks add textural interest to the exterior.

This page, above, the swimming pool and patio area are an art deco feast for the eyes.

Below, the Arizona Biltmore stands like an oasis against the background of desert and mountains.

CALIFORNIA

The state of California offers a range of climate and topographical variety unequalled on the continent. It can boast 1,200 miles of coastline on the magnificent and changeable Pacific Ocean and counter that with the soaring peaks of the Sierra Nevada Mountains. It has deserts as arid as the Sahara itself and lush green forests of ancient redwoods where rain is the rule and sunshine the exception. It has sprawling modern metropolises and sleepy, old-fashioned villages. For every bustling population center there is a slice of the most magnificent wilderness imaginable; for every mile of freeway there is an untravelled path through virgin forest or along sandy beach. It has the year-round summer of its southern beaches and some of the best skiing in the West around the glacial Lake Tahoe. And when the sun sets on the continental United States, its last fiery glow warms the golden California coast.

Visitors have been discovering California's beauty over and again for centuries. It began with the conquistadores, *and indeed the Spanish influence on the state can be seen in its missions and the mission architecture that abounds there. Of the state's Grand Hotels, the Santa Barbara Biltmore gives evidence of that heritage.*

When in 1513 Vasco Nunez de Balboa first sighted the Pacific Ocean and claimed all the shoreline touched by it for the Spanish Crown, the California territory began its three centuries under Spanish influence. In the course of the next few decades, searchers for El Dorado, *the legendary city of gold, ventured into California under the leadership of Francisco Vasquez de Coronado. Coronado's men did not find* El Dorado, *there or anywhere else, but they did play a significant part in charting the unknown territory and paving the way for further settlement. Today, Coronado's name is remembered by the peninsula south of San Diego on which stands the fabulous Hotel del Coronado. And, of course, the gold was there after all, although considerably farther north and in somewhat different form than the* conquistadores *imagined.*

Northern California, in fact, was of little interest to the Spanish. It was the Russians, in search of animal pelts and fishing grounds, who established themselves in the northern region in the early Nineteenth Century. Fort Ross and the Russian River, both in Mendocino County, are reminders of that presence. In general, though, the last frontier of the American continent remained a Spanish possession until the 1830s, and then a Mexican colony until 1848, when the Treaty of Guadalupe Hidalgo ceded the territory to the United States.

California was admitted to the Union as the thirty-first state just in time for the discovery of gold at Sutter's Mill in the northern portion of the state. That began the Gold Rush, the influx of the Forty-niners, and the final argument in favor of extending the railroads out to the Pacific Coast thus rang resoundingly clear.

The rest is history. Its splendid climate and the irrigation of acres and acres of semidesert made California the garden of the United States, with the Southern Pacific and other great railroads carrying its produce to the East Coast and all the states between.

The establishment of the movie, and later television, industries in Hollywood brought wealth and a wealthy class to California the likes of which this country had never before known.

And yet, surprisingly, this Golden State boasts few hotels in the grand manner. The reasons behind this can, undoubtedly, be traced to the very influences that brought about California's growth. At a time when the Grand Hotels of the Virginias and the South were becoming established, California was Mexican territory. Later, when it had gained statehood, there was a rough-and-ready frontier spirit, hardly the milieu in which a gracious, European-style vacation resort would flourish.

And when the money, and the leisure to spend it at a resort hotel, had been achieved, those who did not take the European Grand Tour after an Atlantic crossing aboard a luxury liner chose instead to invest in palatial mansions on a private scale. The California coastline abounds with magnificent private homes rivalling the great mansions of Europe; the desert areas around Palm Springs are dotted with million-dollar real estate.

Still, there are a few of them, the Grand Hotels. Those that remain today, two overlooking the Pacific and one nestled at the foot of the Sierra Nevada Mountains, exemplify the Golden Age of the Grand Hotels as well as anything I can imagine.

THE BROADMOOR

Right, elegance is the keynote in this public room in The Broadmoor.

Below, the stately splendor of this outdoor fountain welcomes guests to The Broadmoor and sets the regal tone.

ARIZONA BILTMORE

Right, the lobby of the Arizona Biltmore is warm and inviting. Earth colors cast a glow on the finely detailed pilasters in this art deco masterwork.

Below, surrounded by palms and desert shrubbery, the Arizona Biltmore stands as a monument to modern American design.

SANTA BARBARA BILTMORE

This page, white stucco archways and red quarry tile frame an interior courtyard of the Santa Barbara Biltmore.

Following page, the swimming pool at the Santa Barbara Biltmore; the Pacific Ocean lies beyond.

HOTEL DEL CORONADO

Like an anthology of Victorian architectural detail, the Hotel del Coronado stands majestic in the sunshine.

Left, down to the smallest detail, the splendor of Victorian design abounds in the hotel. This milk-glass lamp casts a warm glow on the wood and glass-enclosed wine case.

Below, crystal draped chandeliers recall an opulent past in this grand ballroom.

Facing page, the famed Victorian pool house at the Hotel del Coronado—a landmark of the Hotel and a genuine architectural treasure.

Facing page, no setting for a hotel could be grander than the cathedral heights of the Sierra Nevada Range. The rustic beauty of The Ahwahnee Hotel is evident even against those purple mountains' majesty.

This page, the swimming pool and patio at The Ahwahnee. The sun shines through a break in the canopy of trees that encircle the Hotel.

Santa Barbara Biltmore

SANTA BARBARA, CALIFORNIA

"The fairest jewel in the entire chain," is how John McEntee Bowman, former president of the Biltmore Hotels Corporation, described the Santa Barbara Biltmore. Set on the oceanfront, flanked by palm and cypress trees, with a backdrop of the Santa Ynez Mountains, the Biltmore presents a harmony of Spanish, Portuguese, and Moorish styles. The setting could well be Corsica rather than California.

Located in the charming Montecito district of Santa Barbara, the Biltmore was constructed on the site of the estate of copper king James Douglas. It opened on December 16, 1927, and has thereafter catered to a discriminating clientele. Guests appreciated Reginald Johnson's sensitive architecture—the two-story stucco design, the low, sloping red-tiled roofs, the arcades and curving stairways, arbors, patios, walkways, and carved wood and grillework. Johnson, also the designer of the renowned La Valencia Hotel in La Jolla, California, was one of the foremost architects of his day and the first from the West Coast to receive a medal from the Architectural League of New York.

The Biltmore originally operated on a preferential card system: A beige card was given to valued guests, a blue card to even more valued guests, and a pink card to VIPs. In the early days, The Coral Casino Club, the private cabana across the road from the main hotel, was the exclusive domain of pink cardholders. Presenting one's card to the *maître d'hotel* insured preferred seating in the restaurant. Originally, a coat and tie were required even for a drink at the bar; today, jackets are still necessary after six in the evening.

During World War II, the hotel became a military redistribution station. At war's end, it was completely redecorated, and in 1946 Gardner Daily, prominent architect and designer of The Coral Casino Club, built an addition. In 1976, the Marriott Corporation acquired the hotel.

The Biltmore today houses 176 guest rooms in low, two-story buildings and cottages. The bedrooms are tastefully and elegantly furnished—television sets are concealed in custom-built armoires. As befits a Grand Hotel, the Biltmore features spacious rooms and generously proportioned beds, both larger than the standard.

The Coral Casino Club has an Olympic-sized swimming pool and direct access to ocean and private beach. For members, there is a private dining room and cocktail lounge.

For diners at the hotel, the handsome dining room overlooks the gardens, and *al fresco* dining on the patio is featured in season.

The hotel is a fitting addition to Santa Barbara. This Southern California city prides itself on its successful blending of setting, climate, and architecture. To the west, visitors may marvel at the vastness of the Pacific Ocean and the view of the Channel Islands; to the east, there is the dramatic panorama of the low-lying Santa Ynez Mountains. Architecturally the city is restricted to Mission Revival and Spanish Colonial styles. The area has one of the most stringent urban planning laws in the nation; an Architectural Board of Review has final say on almost everything that is built. The result is a stylistic harmony and community pride in the reintroduction of its Spanish origin. Those who think these restrictions go too far frequently gripe, "If it has tile roofs and stucco walls, it belongs in Santa Barbara."

Santa Barbara's attitude toward its architectural unity can be traced directly to the June 29, 1925 earthquake, which virtually destroyed the business district. Before the quake, especially toward the end of the Nineteenth Century, Santa Barbara was inundated with Victorian-style buildings. In the aftermath of the quake, the community determined to rebuild

Facing page, the Santa Barbara Biltmore, surrounded by towering palms with the Santa Ynez Mountains visible in the distance.

This page, the California Mission style is evident in this view of the Santa Barbara Biltmore lobby. Glazed tiles, wrought-iron fixtures, and unadorned archways are featured.

Facing page, the low profile of the two-story hotel buildings is typical of the local architecture. Tile roofs and textured stucco exterior walls bespeak the town's Spanish Colonial heritage.

the city with an emphasis on its Spanish heritage. Within a few weeks the Architectural Board of Review was formed; and within eight months it had approved about 2,000 plans for new construction—virtually all in the preferred style. The Santa Barbara Biltmore followed this mandate.

Today regulations in Santa Barbara are even more stringent: There is a ban on billboards and restrictions on building heights—they rarely exceed four stories. The downtown area has been transformed into a carless mall, and the El Pueblo Viejo ordinance limits all buildings to "California adobe type."

Facing page, this lovely interior court is lushly planted and meticulously cared for.

This page, *right*, the dining room at the Santa Barbara Biltmore. Its timbered ceiling stands out in dramatic contrast to the white walls.

Below, floor-to-ceiling arched windows tie together this cool lobby interior with the sun-dappled garden in the courtyard outside.

Hotel del Coronado

CORONADO, CALIFORNIA

The Victorian splendor of the Hotel del Coronado is visible from miles away. As the traveler approaches the peak of the San Diego-Coronado Bridge, the gingerbread facade and the turreted and cupolated roof dominate the view. The structure is considered one of the most extravagantly conceived seaside buildings in the United States, and rightly so. Its tall pillars and elegant domes are touched with the elegance and craftsmanship of yesterday.

Before 1870, the land on which the Hotel stands was considered of little worth; the 4,100 acres that constitute the Coronado Peninsula were valued at $1,000. But by 1885, when Elisha Babcock, a retired railroad executive, and H. L. Story, of the Story and Clark Piano Company, purchased it, the price was $110,000.

Babcock knew how spectacular the site was, and he was determined to use it well. He planned to build a resort hotel that would be the talk of the West. Construction was soon started, the rough drawings of architects James, Merritt, and Watson Reid, serving as the builder's guide. (Formal architectural plans never were drafted!) A railroad spur and a ferry system were set up to deliver lumber, other building materials, fixtures, furniture, and workmen. The Hotel was laboriously constructed of wood at a time when San Diego had neither wood nor skilled workers, both having to be brought in from San Francisco.

In February 1888, the Hotel del Coronado opened. It was not yet finished, but the structure was so unique in design and concept—its size alone made it a wonder—that thousands came from all over the country to see it. Two years later, in 1890, the Hotel was finally completed—a five-story, 400-room, Victorian structure on thirty-three seaside acres within sight of the Mexican-American border.

The main dining room, The Crown Room, is distinguished by an arched ceiling made of natural sugar pine, the sections fitted together with wooden pegs. There are no posts, no interior supports. For years it had the distinction of being the largest room in the United States without supporting pillars. The damask on the walls matches the carpet on the floor; the elaborate corona lighting fixtures are world famous. The Grand Ballroom overlooks the ocean, and the enormous chandeliers, hanging from the thirty-one foot ceiling, rival those of the Pavilion at Brighton, England. Although minor structural changes have been made, The Crown Room and The Grand Ballroom have changed very little since opening day.

Today the main building has 380 guest rooms, each with a private bath (compared to only 75 bathrooms in 1888). Originally the rooms had working fireplaces, but they were replaced with steam heat in 1897. The gas lighting has always been purely ornamental; the electrical system was one of the world's largest when it was first installed.

Since its opening the Hotel del Coronado has entertained many distinguished guests from the worlds of society, business, and politics, among them eight Presidents. Astors, Vanderbilts, Tiffanys, and Armours have graced its halls. And it was at the Hotel that Edward XIII first met Wallis Simpson. The long list of guests from the world of show business includes Charlie Chaplin, Ramon Novarro, Jimmy Durante, and Robert Taylor. Dozens of movies have featured the hotel, perhaps best remembered is *Some Like It Hot,* with Marilyn Monroe.

On December 13, 1970, the Hotel del Coronado became an official State of California landmark. The commemorative plaque reads: "This Victorian hotel, built in 1888, is one of America's largest wooden buildings. Few seaside resort hotels of this significant architectural style remain in America." And in May 1977 the Hotel became a National Historic Landmark.

Facing page, well known for its delightful Victorian detail, the Hotel del Coronado has a storybook quality about it.

This page, right, arches and railings, dormers and cupolas, turrets and gingerbread trim—all contribute to the splendid jumble that is the Hotel del Coronado.

Below, and facing page, the white railed porches which run along the face of the Hotel give guests privacy with a view. The splendid cupolas which cap the building have brick-red shingled roofs that are visible from miles away.

The Ahwahnee Hotel

YOSEMITE, CALIFORNIA

The history of The Ahwahnee Hotel began a million years ago, when glaciers carved out the Yosemite Valley. When the ice cap receded what remained was a dramatic region of towering stone walls, alpine meadows, and numerous lakes and streams. With its rugged stone walls rising amidst the shadow of the Royal Arches, The Ahwahnee Hotel is an imposing sight in that spectacular valley.

When construction of the first all-weather road to the Yosemite area was announced for 1926, National Park Service authorities became aware that there were no suitable winter lodgings for the travelers who would use the new highway. At one time the valley had been serviced by four hotels, but by the early 1920s only the very dilapidated Sentinel Hotel survived. The village of Kennyville was selected as the location for a park hotel because of the superb view it offered of Yosemite Falls, Half Dome, and Glacier Point.

Shortly before the site had been chosen, the two leading Yosemite concessionaires merged to form the Yosemite Park and Curry Company. The Director of the National Park Service, Stephen T. Mather, pushed for quality accommodations. Yosemite was his favorite national park and he wanted a great influx of visitors to help him justify and obtain congressional funds for its development. Mather did succeed in getting Washington to upgrade the old stagecoach roads and construct a park service headquarters, a post office, and photo stores, but he also wanted the best roads and trails, the widest publicity, and a luxury hotel that would attract influential people.

An agreement was signed with the Curry Company, stipulating that the National Park Service would own the land and structure, and set the rates for a Hotel; the Company would build the lodge, furnish it, and operate it under a renewable twenty-year contract. A 100-bedroom building was proposed with an estimated cost of $300,000. The dining room and lobby would be large enough to hold 500 to 1,000 people. Plans were put forward to build cottages as well, these for 100 additional guests. But as The Ahwahnee neared completion—$1 million and 92 rooms later—the magnitude of the plans was reduced.

Construction of the Hotel is a story in itself. Gilbert Stanley Underwood, an eminent architect from Los Angeles, was selected to draw plans for a "hotel that fits the environment." He designed a massive, three-wing, six-story structure of native granite and of concrete stained to look like wood. Although the Curry Company was pleased with the exterior, they considered the plans for the interior impractical and demanded drastic revisions. After months of wrangling, Mr. Underwood offered new plans, which were approved late in March 1926. Construction began in June and the cornerstone was laid on August 1, 1927. What transpired in the intervening months involved a tremendous challenge, a fair amount of bureaucratic interference, and what seemed at times like overwhelming odds.

Contractor James L. McLaughlin had expected to complete the Hotel for $525,000, but within a few months of ground-breaking, estimated costs had risen to $800,000, and by completion date the cost would reach $1 million. The opening was seven months late. Delays and cost overruns were apparently the result of bureaucratic squabbling. Among McLaughlin's great achievements, however, was the transportation of building material to the site. For thirteen months, seven days a week, more than 1,000 tons of steel and 5,000 tons of stone were carried over rough roads on six-wheeled trucks.

A private celebration opened The Ahwahnee on July 14, 1927; the Hotel welcomed the public two days later. But the problems had still not been resolved. At the last minute it was discovered that the guest rooms that were situated directly above the entrance were unbear-

Facing page, the rugged beauty of native stone is put to excellent use in The Ahwahnee Hotel. Stone pillars flank exterior walls made of concrete, cast and colored to resemble wood.

ably noisy. A new entrance was immediately planned on the north side of the building, with a long covered walkway. As Hil Oehlmann, general manager of the Curry Company, recalled, "With opening date set and the guests invited, the new construction was so hurriedly executed that it is only a slight exaggeration to state that the carpenters were but a few feet ahead of the painters, and the painters almost collided with the first arriving guests."

The gala opening was in any event a great success. The next morning, however, was a management nightmare. It seems the fifty special guests—or some of them at least—had helped themselves to mementos of the occasion: pewter inkstands, ashtrays, handloomed blankets and bedspreads, and even the prized Indian baskets that had been displayed on the mezzanine. Security precautions were taken before the first paying guests registered, but it was a clear case of locking the barn door after the VIPs had gotten away.

Not everyone was pleased with The Ahwahnee. The American democratic spirit rebelled against such promotional blurbs as, "The Ahwahnee is designed quite frankly for people who know the delights of luxurious living, and to whom the artistic excellence and the material comforts of the environment are important." Many considered such snobbery inappropriate to a public park facility. The Ahwahnee lost $75,000 within its first six months of operation. The staff was reduced, and rates of rooms for the maids and chauffeurs of guests were lowered. With the coming of the Depression, business plummeted even further. The staff was cut a second time and salaries reduced. Only the continuing patronage of some wealthy families kept the Hotel solvent.

The Depression ended the snob appeal of The Ahwahnee. The Curry Company, hungry for business, launched a massive public relations campaign. Ansel Adams, the now-famous photographer of the Yosemite Valley, was hired to take pictures of the Hotel and the setting. Yet business continued to be marginal. Net profits in 1933 were down to $1,495, and park attendance dropped from a high of 450,000 in 1916 to 296,000 in 1933. Business finally picked up when winter sports facilities were added to the Park.

During World War II, The Ahwahnee served as a convalescent hospital for sailors. Unfortunately, its wartime lodgers left the place in a bad state: the wildflower meadows were destroyed; plaster walls and pillars were damaged; built-in chests of drawers required repair; and the flooring, which had been badly gouged, had to be completely relaid. Much of the furniture had also been damaged, either in storage or in transit. The Navy lease ended June 30, 1946, and by December of that same year, The Ahwahnee, under the management of the Curry Company, was once again open to the public. A new feature dominating the lobby was a large lamp made from a Native American basket, and in the Great Lounge an enormous wall painting of a geometric design graced the area over the mantel.

From 1969 to 1973, management of the Hotel underwent a series of changes. The Shasta Corporation bought a large block of Curry Company stock in 1969; they, in turn, were acquired in 1971 by a private concern called the United States Natural Resources Company. Two years later the holdings were transferred to MCA, Inc., and that corporation poured $400,000 into maintenance and restoration of the Hotel.

Today the central focus of the Hotel interior is the Great Lounge, a vast but friendly room with a huge fireplace, comfortable seating, area rugs, beamed ceilings from which hang cast-iron chandeliers, and ten ceiling-to-floor windows topped with stained glass panels designed by Jeanette Dyer Spencer.

The lobby floor features six striking geometric figures set in tile mosaic. The elevator lobby is dominated by a vivid basket mural above the fireplace, and the tops of the bedroom walls are ornamented with narrow borders of Native American geometrics. Ten-foot windows on the south side of the dining room offer views of Glacier Point, and Yosemite Falls can be seen from the great window at the west alcove. The dining room is lined with bark covered sugar-pine columns; the pilasters, trusses, and rafters are of natural wood.

Of all the hotels we have visited in the pages of this book The Ahwahnee is the most remote in location, the most rustic in decor. But it is, in a very real sense, a grand resort hotel. Surrounded by one of our most stunning of natural resources, Yosemite National Park, it offers vacationers a truly special kind of grandeur.

The timbered ceiling is double height to accommodate the handsome ten-foot windows from which diners can see Yosemite Park's Glacier Point.

Epilogue

In the course of preparing this book we found several hotels that were abandoned or whose buildings were no longer in use as hotels. Of the half dozen we visited, The Castaneda Hotel at Las Vegas, New Mexico, and The Phoenix resort, formerly The Montezuma, at nearby Las Vegas Hot Springs, are vivid examples of Grand Hotels whose histories are now completely past.

The Castaneda Hotel is last listed in *Western Accommodations Directory* in 1948. It was not an imposing building, but it deserves mention because of its railroad-type architecture, a style rarely seen today. It was located at the foot of the Sangre de Cristo Mountains, part of the Rocky Mountain range, an area of great scenic beauty. The city of Las Vegas, forty miles from the state capital at Santa Fe, grew from an old stopover on the Santa Fe Railroad to an important trading center. It is now a city of a bit less than 8,000 people and the demand for one, let alone two, Grand Hotels no longer exists.

The Montezuma Hotel, at the hot springs ten miles away, is a castle-like structure that once attracted a distinguished clientele, visitors from all over the world come to the area to enjoy the curative waters. The Hotel burned twice and finally closed because of declining popularity. It was subsequently used for a variety of purposes; it once housed a seminary, but it now appears to be abandoned.

A 1902 announcement for the Las Vegas and Hot Springs Electric Railway, Light and Power Company reads:

Ten miles of an electric railway is now in operation between The Castaneda Hotel, East Las Vegas, and The Montezuma, Las Vegas Hot Springs. The finest climate and the most beautiful scenic route in the world.

Facing page, sunlight leaks through the open archways of this deserted arcade of The Castaneda Hotel.

The two-story railroad structure of The Castaneda is evident in these two views. It consists of a central building with two right-angle wings extending out to flank the front lawn, now gone to seed.

Above, viewed from the distance, The Montezuma Hotel appears to be a rambling and somewhat miscellaneous collection of building wings.

Below, a back garden of the deserted hotel, overgrown and the building in disrepair.

Facing page, a once-proud facade of The Montezuma, complete with turret and handsome stonework.

Directory of Hotels

The Ahwahnee Hotel
Yosemite National Park, CA 95389
209-373-4171

Arizona Biltmore
P.O. Box 2290
Phoenix, AZ 85002
602-955-6600
800-228-3000

The Boca Raton Hotel and Club
P.O. Box 225
Camino Real
Boca Raton, FL 33432
305-395-3000
800-432-0150 in Florida

The Breakers
South County Road
Palm Beach, FL 33480
305-655-6611

The Broadmoor
Colorado Springs, CO 80901
303-634-7711

Buck Hill Inn
Buck Hill Falls, PA 18323
717-595-7441
800-233-8113

The Cloister
Sea Island, GA 31561
912-638-3611
800-841-3223

Grand Hotel
Mackinac Island, MI 49757
906-847-3331

The Grand Hotel
Point Clear, AL 36564
205-928-9201

The Greenbrier
White Sulphur Springs, WV 24986
304-536-1110
800-624-6070

The Homestead
Hot Springs, VA 24445
703-839-5500
800-336-5771

Hotel del Coronado
1500 Orange Avenue
Coronado, CA 92118
714-435-6611

Hotel Hershey
Routes 322 and 422
Hershey, PA 17033
717-533-2171

The Lake Placid Club
Lake Placid, NY 12946
518-523-3361
800-342-9501 in New York State

Marriott Santa Barbara Biltmore
1260 Channel Drive
Santa Barbara, CA 93108
805-969-2261   800-228-9290

Mountain View House
Whitefield, NH 03598
603-837-2511

Pocono Manor Inn and Golf Club
Pocono Manor, PA 18349
717-839-7111

Wentworth-by-the-Sea
New Castle, NH 03801
603-436-3100

Whiteface Inn and Golf Club
Lake Placid, NY 12946
518-523-2551

Bibliography

BOOKS

American Automobile Association. *AAA Regional Accommodations Directories.* Falls Church, VA: 1948–1960.

Amory, Cleveland. *Last Resorts.* New York: Harper & Row, 1952.

Bancroft, Peggy. *Ringing Axes and Rocking Chairs.* Mountainhome, PA.: Barret Friendly Library, 1974.

Hepburn, Andrew. *Great Resorts of North America.* New York: Doubleday, 1965.

Ingalls, Fay. *The Valley Road.* Cleveland: World Publishing, 1940.

Ludy, Robert, M.D. *Historic Hotels of the World.* New York: David McKay, 1927.

Myrick, David F. *New Mexico's Railroads.* Golden, Colorado: Colorado Railroad Museum, 1970.

Roads to Cibola: What to See in New Mexico. 1929.

PAMPHLETS AND BROCHURES

The Arizona Biltmore Hotel: A History and Guide. Oak Park, IL: Frank Lloyd Wright Foundation, 1931.

Dewey, Godfrey. *Sixty Years of Lake Placid Club.* Reprint of a lecture, 1955.

The Dodge Family and Their Hotel. Courier Printing, 1973.

Geiger, Helen M. *The Broadmoor Story.* Herman Raymond Printing Co., 1968.

Hershey. Western Publishing Co., 1974.

Resort Management Guide. June 1977.

Rivan, Gen. Hugh W. and McKenzie, Mary. *The Shore Owner's Association of Lake Placid.* 1973.

Sargent, Shirley. *The Ahwahnee.* California: Yosemite Park and Curry Co., 1977.

Warner Digest of Distinguished Resorts, 1976–77. New York: Robert Warner Publications.

Index